Cambridge Elements ☰

Elements in Critical Issues in Teacher Education
edited by
Tony Loughland
University of New South Wales
Andy Gao
University of New South Wales
Hoa T. M. Nguyen
University of New South Wales

INTERCULTURALITY, CRITICALITY AND REFLEXIVITY IN TEACHER EDUCATION

Fred Dervin
University of Helsinki

CAMBRIDGE
UNIVERSITY PRESS

Shaftesbury Road, Cambridge CB2 8EA, United Kingdom

One Liberty Plaza, 20th Floor, New York, NY 10006, USA

477 Williamstown Road, Port Melbourne, VIC 3207, Australia

314–321, 3rd Floor, Plot 3, Splendor Forum, Jasola District Centre,
New Delhi – 110025, India

103 Penang Road, #05–06/07, Visioncrest Commercial, Singapore 238467

Cambridge University Press is part of Cambridge University Press & Assessment,
a department of the University of Cambridge.

We share the University's mission to contribute to society through the pursuit of
education, learning and research at the highest international levels of excellence.

www.cambridge.org
Information on this title: www.cambridge.org/9781009302814

DOI: 10.1017/9781009302777

First published 2023

A catalogue record for this publication is available from the British Library.

ISBN 978-1-009-30281-4 Paperback
ISSN 2755-1202 (online)
ISSN 2755-1199 (print)

Interculturality, Criticality and Reflexivity in Teacher Education

Elements in Critical Issues in Teacher Education

DOI: 10.1017/9781009302777
First published online: February 2023

Fred Dervin
University of Helsinki

Author for correspondence: Fred Dervin, fred.dervin@helsinki.fi

Abstract: Preparing teachers to work with and for diversity in their classrooms and beyond is an objective that seems to be globally accepted in pre-service and in-service teacher education. However, what diversity means, what it entails and how to engage with diverse individuals in educational contexts can take on multiple shapes in different parts of the world. This Element suggests that the multifaceted and polysemic notion of interculturality could be useful to unthink and rethink (ad infinitum) working with diverse people in education. The Element surveys the different meanings and ideologies attached to the notion, using a multilingual perspective to do so. Recent research published internationally on the topic and its companions such as multiculturalism is also reviewed. The main addition to the field is a critical and reflexive perspective which is proposed for teacher educators, (students) teachers and researchers. The proposal draws from Dervin's most up-to-date theoretical and pedagogical work.

This Element also has a video abstract: www.cambridge.org/dervin

Keywords: interculturality, teacher education, critical thinking, reflexivity, interdisciplinarity

ISBNs: 9781009302814 (PB), 9781009302777 (OC)
ISSNs: 2755-1202 (online), 2755-1199 (print)

Contents

1 Reflexive Introduction

Objectives

- To justify the need for a text on interculturality for teacher education;
- To understand what the Element is about and who it is aimed at;
- To reflect on the complexities and polysemy of the notion of interculturality.

Reflect Before Reading the Section

- Why did you pick up this Element? What kind of knowledge are you looking for? Why is interculturality important to you as a (future) teacher, a teacher educator and/or a researcher?
- What comes to mind when you hear the word *interculturality* in English and in other languages? What is it about?
- Who does the notion refer to concretely? When you say *intercultural communication*, for example, who do you imagine to be involved?
- Is the notion of interculturality omnipresent in your own institution and context? Are other similar words used? What do they mean in comparison and why do you think they are also in use?
- How much is interculturality embedded in teacher training and education in your country? What are the expected outcomes of learning about it?
- Finally, reflect on your own experiences of interculturality as a teacher and as an individual. Pick three examples and reflect on these questions: how would you describe your experience? Why did you pick these three examples? How relevant and important have they been in your life? How much have they shaped you?

Preamble: What This Element Is About and for Whom

The notion of interculturality, and its derivatives and companions such as *intercultural communication*, *multiculturalism* and *transculturality*, is multifaceted. It can be defined, understood and used in many different ways in different walks of life. At times, it is not even circumscribed but used as an 'automaton' to refer to, for example, 'meeting people from abroad', 'meeting cultures' or 'clashing with other cultures'. Usually the way we engage with the broad range of terms denoting interculturality relates to the way we have been made to think about *us* and *them*, to compare our 'country'/'culture' with other 'countries'/'cultures' and to locate our own position in the global world. Foreign and domestic politics, the media, social media, the arts, our acquaintances, friends and family, as well as education (amongst other aspects) have all shaped the way we see and 'do' interculturality, often in unstable ways. One day we might think that 'Brits are this or that', uttering a coarse generalization, and the next day, talking to a British individual, we might make a statement that counters the stereotype we held the previous day. One day we might face discrimination in another country, and start being sensitive to the issue of racism in our own context upon return. Finally, after reading a media report about the plight of refugees in another part of the world, we might change our own views on the issue of migration. As educators, all of these elements also influence us in the way we think, unthink, rethink and do interculturality in our classrooms and beyond. As a central component of any society, education interacts indirectly or directly with the ways people are perceived and treated outside schools. As such, education is a place of otherness par excellence; being confronted by the other and othering (considering the other through limited lenses) is a common experience in schools. One could say that the other, *us versus them*, is part and parcel of education and that interculturality is inevitable. However, what the notion means and how it can be applied to the work of teachers is multifaceted around the world. The way it is introduced in teacher education might also differ immensely. For example, I am writing from Finland, a country famed for its education and whose teachers seem to be revered around the world. In this context, teacher education does not aim to equip future teachers with a few 'tricks' to engage with interculturality but to help them build up enough criticality and reflexivity around the notion to be able to deal with the complex intercultural situations that they will face when they start working with diverse individuals in their classrooms, schools and beyond. As a teacher educator myself, I do not provide pre-service teachers with 'ready-made' knowledge about what interculturality is, what it does or what to do about it but I 'learn' with them how to consider the notion from multiple scientific, economic-political and ideological angles so we can multiply and adapt our (re-)actions to it. We thus acquaint ourselves with global research on the notion (from 'dominating' models to lesser-known perspectives), try out ideas in groups and with future teachers from Finland and other parts of the world (e.g. Peng & Dervin, 2022; Chen & Dervin, 2023), and reflect on interculturality as a notion that deserves opening up again and again. Preparing in-service teachers for interculturality in the Finnish context is not about providing them with 'miraculous tools' but about empowering them to make decisions about interculturality together with others in different contexts and situations. One recurring argument made in this Element is that interculturality as a phenomenon is 'fluid' (e.g. Holliday, 2010; Dervin & R'boul, 2022) and that dealing with it educationally and academically requires 'dissolving' the way we have been made to think about it.

I have written the Element not to provide easy recipes to 'doing' interculturality in teacher education but for us to reflect further on the complexities of engaging with a notion that appears to be central in our current fragmented and conflictual worlds with, for example, a war in Europe, economic crises, increasing social and racial injustice, and geopolitical polarization. I use the word 'world' in the plural on purpose, as a first reminder that we need to think of *us* and *them* as complex entities as we engage with interculturality. Considering the grave situation of today – which derives from past issues – interculturality should be taken seriously.

This is the main message of this Element: as educators, there is a need for us to consider the idea of interculturality from multiple perspectives, to examine and revise consciously and constantly our own takes on the notion. Interculturality is not a monolith and as soon as we start interacting with others around the notion, we notice that we do not necessarily share the same meanings, connotations and even values about interculturality. For some of us, interculturality might be about 'cultures', about the 'international'; for others, it could be about 'migrants from certain parts of the world', 'Indigenous people', 'races' and/or 'ethnicities' – or a mix of all of these. What is more, when it comes to what we are supposed to be aiming at 'interculturally', different ideological constructs might also apply. Here I use the concept of *ideology* not in a negative way but to refer to what, for example, education tells us is the 'right' thing to do (Roucek, 1944). As far as interculturality is concerned, one might promote *tolerance, respect, sensitivity, open-mindedness, brotherhood, unity,* but also *social justice* and/or *equality* (amongst others). All these terms can also be indefinite and ambiguous in the ways they are used in different contexts and especially in different languages.

Like most scholars and educators, I have my own beliefs about what interculturality could be and how to 'do' it. Throughout my career, I have kept and modified certain aspects of its definition. Some of these elements were influenced directly by my reading, my research (interviews, focus groups and ethnographies of thousands of people in different parts of the world), my learning in the classroom as an educator, my engagement with junior and senior scholars from around the world and my own life experiences. Other aspects of my take on interculturality might be more related to worldviews and ideologies that were passed on to me without me being fully aware of them. I could share with you what I think interculturality is and how you should do it. I have done so in the past, preferring a so-called postmodern, liquid and anti-essentialist form of interculturality, which puts the emphasis on co-constructions, identity (re-)negotiations, power and processes of encountering (see e.g. Dervin, 2016; Dervin, 2022a; Dervin et al., 2022). But I don't feel that my role in this Element is to put forward this 'Western' perspective, which is somewhat dominating research today (e.g. Dervin & Jacobsson, 2022). I would not want to give the impression that interculturality is *one* and that my way of engaging with it is the only and right way, or that there is some kind of universal way of doing it in research and education. As such, in Finland, discussions of interculturality tend to revolve around immigrants and refugees, and 'elite' educational internationalization. In 2022, the key topics of *diversity, social justice* and *anti-racism* seem to dominate the Finnish educational context and teacher education/training. Speaking to different colleagues and teachers from around the world, I notice that their takes on these terms are many and varied and that there does not seem to be a unified way of engaging with them. In recent years, I have also worked extensively in the Chinese context, both with scholars working on, for example, language and intercultural education (e.g. Tan et al., 2022) and on Chinese Minzu ('ethnic') education (e.g. Dervin & Yuan, 2021). These two different strands of 'interculturality' have their own specific mixed discourses, methods and practices, with very few intersections. It means that when I work on Minzu education with my colleagues, we do not use the same terms and references as when I work with Chinese language specialists. Similarly, the educational objectives set differ. For example, the language and intercultural education strand focuses on tolerance and global-mindedness (amongst other aspects), while the Minzu education one, which focuses on the education of the diverse fifty-six Minzu groups of Mainland China, looks into fostering a sense of 'diversity in unity' in students and providing students from less-developed areas with opportunities through affirmative actions. In this Element, I often use examples from Mainland China to either illustrate points that I make or to make us think further about the need to consider ways of engaging with interculturality beyond the 'West'. My experiences with China have been the most significant ones in helping me to unthink and rethink the notion. I have also cooperated extensively with colleagues from France, Malaysia and the United States, where the terms used and objectives set can also differ. So, promoting my own beliefs about interculturality, especially in relation to how we could 'do' it, is out of the question here. Again, I am more interested in going on a journey of discovery with you.

As a consequence of the points made earlier, I need to say that this Element will not train you to 'do' interculturality 'properly' since this adverb could mean different things in many different contexts. Instead, following the Finnish trend to stimulate criticality and reflexivity in teacher education, the Element will support you in reflecting critically about how you 'do' it, the meaning(s) you give to the notion and the lifelong changes that you can make to it. Depending on the context and interests, the Element can be used by teacher educators, pre-service and in-service teachers and scholars involved in researching interculturality. Readers interested in inclusive education and language education, for example, might also find the Element stimulating. Both subfields have contributed directly and indirectly to scholarship on the notion (e.g. Ferguson-Patrick & Jolliffe, 2018; Cobb & Bower, 2021). Since interculturality is included in many educational and academic discussions surrounding teacher education, I will only make passing remarks on these subfields so as not to 'overcrowd' the Element.

I have now been addressing you, my reader, many times. But as I am writing these words, I am wondering who is it that I am talking to. Who are the heterogenous 'ears' that are listening to me now? As a writer, I need to imagine who you are. You could be from any part of the world, from Ghana to Bolivia, from Norway to Oman, from Tajikistan to China. You could be a scholar, a novice researcher, a colleague and friend, a teacher in primary school, a teacher educator, in-service and pre-service teachers from all levels of the curriculum. You might work for a private institution, a public/state one, an NGO or a professional development centre. You might be a Christian, a Mormon, a Sikh or an atheist. You might have travelled the world or never left your country, your town or your village. Some of you might have several passports. Some of you might work in another country, in one of your countries, online. Some of you might speak several languages and dialects, write in two different languages or understand five languages orally. Finally, some of you will have read hundreds of books and articles on the topic of interculturality, while others might have just taken a short course on how to develop intercultural competence, for example. These selective (and limited) categories represent a good reminder to me as the one writing this Element and to you, my extremely complex range of readers: our interaction mediated by paper or a screen is also very much intercultural.

No one would ever be able to publish a book that addresses all these different identities, profiles and needs. Different readers will have their special interests and priorities. As soon as a book is published in English today, it is aimed at the whole world. My duty here is to consider that you are all from different parts of the world, that you have different statuses (teacher educators, in-service and pre-service teachers. . .) with different starting points concerning interculturality and that I must take this consistently into account in problematizing how we could deal with interculturality in teacher education. Some of my own (restricted) beliefs will most likely pop up here and there in the Element. Use these moments as opportunities to reflect on why I could be writing in a such or such way or why I might make a given point. In general, I would say that the Element is aimed at those of us who (think they) know about interculturality and at those who (think they) don't and who have an interest in teacher education.

Finally, while I consider myself a specialist of interculturality in education, I constantly need to remind myself that I don't know everything about it. Although there is a hierarchy established between me as a writer and you as a reader – I have the 'power to speak', the reader remains silent somewhat – my approach does not consist in *looking down upon you* and in *telling you that you don't know*. Unfortunately, I can't *hear* you as you are reading through the sections: I can't listen to your thoughts, your hesitations, your worries, your disagreements or even your laughter, your tears, your anger. These all matter to me as a writer since in dealing with interculturality as an object of research and education, we need all of these in order to move forward in the way we engage with the notion, to enrich our own knowledge. I have no other choice but to accept the limits of our communication here, hoping that I will hear from some of you one day.

What the Element does is to make us think together, asking questions about the ways we might want to engage with interculturality and change as we experience other voices about it. I also have a special responsibility here: there is often an underground accusatory tone in research on interculturality in teacher education, either about students or teachers themselves. As we shall see in the first section, scholars have often looked at how educators understand and perceive interculturality and categorized them into 'neat' boxes that often impose judgements about educators' take. My task here is not to contribute to this but to explore with you how we could deal with such a complex notion throughout our careers. I will not give the illusion that I have answers to all the questions I will be asking and especially not the illusion that I know how to 'do' and deal with interculturality. This Element is meant to be a safe space where we can ask important questions about a notion that urgently needs to be unpacked and discussed today. So, put the atelophobia (the fear of making mistakes) that many of us experience about interculturality aside and join me on this important journey.

What Is Interculturality?

When people ask me what I do and hear that I am a researcher working on interculturality, they often appear to be confused by the word. A few days ago, a friend of mine asked me this question: 'How would you define interculturality in one sentence?' I replied that it has already taken me twenty years of my life to try to make sense of what it is and how people 'do' it and that one sentence would never be enough to summarize what I found. What is interculturality then, the core object of this Element? I am tempted to say *I don't know any more*. When I started in the field, I used interculturality as a mere synonym for *international*. After twenty years of research, cooperating with people from

Australia, Canada, Estonia, Finland, France, Greece, Iceland, Israel, Mainland China, Malaysia, Norway, Spain, Sweden, the UK and the United States (amongst others), I have shifted my thoughts about the notion in many and varied ways. Defining interculturality for an international audience is, in a way, imposing one's own ideological take on such a polysemic concept. By not defining it here, some of you might think that I am putting an end to potential conversations, as if I were saying 'interculturality is interculturality'. But, in fact, the reason why I don't wish to define it here is to keep it floating, to let diverse voices speak about it, and to let you explore with me interculturality in its different facets in the following sections – first listening to research on interculturality and teacher education published in English in top journals and second getting to reflect together on what it might mean and entail in our respective complex contexts.

The question *what is interculturality?* sounds like a very 'normal' and 'obvious' question to start with (the word is on the cover of this Element). I would argue that other kinds of questions could be more relevant for our purpose. For instance:

– What matters most in the word *inter-cultur-ality*? *Inter-? Culture?* And/ or *-ality*? What do each of these elements mean and refer to, especially when combined? What should be done with the problematic concept of *culture*, which seems to mean everything and nothing at the same time (see Wikan, 2002)? About *inter-*: is it meant to indicate *in-betweenness, mixing, mélange* or something else?
– Why do we (want to) use the notion of interculturality in teacher education? Who urges us directly or indirectly to use this label? Why don't we use *multicultural* or *culturally responsive* instead – two other dominating terms used globally?
– How do people engage with the notion of interculturality (and its compan-ions) around the world? What meanings do they give to them? What concepts and words do they use to explain it or to make it workable (e.g. race, worldview, ethnicity, nationality, diversity)?

Before I continue to discuss the very question of *what is interculturality?* I would like to pause for a few moments to reflect with you on one keyword that comes back again and again in English in education today: *diversity*. A few years ago, I was a member of a Nordic research team entitled Diverse Teachers for Diverse Learners. At the very first meeting, I patiently waited for someone to explain who the label *diverse* referred to since no one had told me what it was meant to signify before the meeting. At the end of the day, no one had voiced what was 'hiding' behind the word. I thus ventured a question: 'Who are we talking about here? We have spent eight hours talking to each other but we have not named the core of the issue that we are discussing: who is diverse?' My question was met with silence and embarrassment. We were all white Nordics in the room. I then said: 'Is the word a substitute for another word? *Migrant* perhaps? *Migrant Teachers for Migrant Learners*?' Most of my colleagues nodded and we quickly moved on to the next topic.

The vast majority of articles dealing with interculturality in education tend to start with a statement like 'Schools have never been as diverse as they are today'. What does the word *diverse* mean here? As you read the sentence, certain images probably came to your mind, and depending on where you work in the world, the people that you pictured might have been very different. Some of us might see 'migrant children from certain parts of the world', 'Indigenous pupils', 'pupils from specific ethnic groups' or 'pupils of different races'. Beyond interculturality, some might picture 'children of different genders', 'different socio-economic backgrounds' and even 'children with special needs'. Maybe a minority of us might just picture any group of students that they have worked with, arguing that *every child is diverse*. This leads us to important questions: what is the border between *intercultural* and *non-intercultural* when the people we refer to as *diverse* can encompass such large groups of people? Who decides what is and what is not intercultural? Here again, the answer would depend on contexts, beliefs and ideologies, and economic-political positions.

Many research articles have tried to understand how researchers and educators understand the idea of diversity in education. For example, Holm and Londen (2010) have noted that the word is used as a synonym for 'immigrant pupils' in Finnish policies and curricula. Liu and Ball (2019: 71) demonstrate how scholars dealing with diversity present 'lists of characteristics such as ethnicity, race, language and social class' – with religious and sexual diversity, for example, being less frequently included. They also share their concern about the overuse of the concept of 'cultural diversity' as a potential substitute for other terms that seem to be avoided such as *race* and *ethnicity*. Fylkesnes (2017) agrees that teacher education researchers do not explicitly define 'cultural diversity', with some using it interchangeably with *multicultural*. Interestingly, in a review of papers engaging with the concept of diversity in teacher education, Rowan et al. (2021: 134) note the systematic presence of the following claims:

1. Diversity (in both student and community populations) is a fact of contemporary life.
2. Diversity makes new, and/or increased and/or difficult demands on today's (still largely homogenous) teaching population, which therefore requires particular or further forms of support/preparation.

3. Teacher educators have a major responsibility for ensuring future teachers are as prepared as possible to work effectively and respectfully with the entire student population.

In general, researchers conclude that diversity is conceptually weak in teacher education research and programmes and that this might impede effective and precise communication between different educational actors and decision makers, for example. In the Element I do make use of the words *diverse* and *diversity* without positioning them clearly. I am doing this on purpose not to impose my own biases on you. I know that many of you will place different entities behind the very words. However, when you come across the words in my writing, try to bear in mind that 1. diversity is always a viewpoint (who defines who as *diverse*? Who is included in it and excluded from it?); 2. diversity is a potential misnomer (one could argue that *everybody is in fact diverse*); 3. diversity is a term that can be a substitute for a word that we might not want to voice (e.g. *race* or *culture*).

After this short and important detour, let's go back to the question of *what is interculturality?* I started my career with the label *intercultural* and have stayed with it ever since. In Finland, my professorship is in *multicultural education* but I have only used the label once in my publications. Politically and in terms of research, these two terms do differ and when I was appointed in multicultural education I panicked somehow: *what to do with this label?* At that time, I thought that it was too 'US-centric' and contained ideologies that I did not necessarily back. A few years after I was appointed, several labels appeared on the Finnish academic 'market': *global, social justice* and *sustainable*. Talking to colleagues from these subfields of education, I realized that we often shared the same research interests and that our ideological take on, for example, *us* and *them*, issues of *communication* and *learning/teaching* were quite similar. Travelling the world to give talks and collect data prior to the 2020 pandemic, I also realized that some colleagues used the notion of interculturality in different ways and that some who referred to their work as being *transcultural* or *global* often shared very similar interests and ideas with me. Over the years I have thus decided to stick to interculturality, although I could have used other terms. What matters in the end is to be very explicit about how one understands the notion when we cooperate with others, to be open and curious about other ways of engaging with it, and to modify our own takes whenever we feel it is possible and needed. I do believe that interculturality as an object of research and education should be itself *interculturalized* to open up to others and, especially, to counter current 'Western-centric' perspectives on the notion (Aman, 2017; R'boul, 2021).

What is interculturality? I would say that interculturality is always in the eye of the beholder and that we should never assume that what it refers to and what it urges people to do in education are in line with what we think and (are asked to) do. Discourses of interculturality always take place in a 'space' that goes well beyond the national and yet they are embedded in glocal (global + local) contexts. I have used the label *intercultural* throughout my career but I feel that I cannot close the door to other labels and other ways of perceiving, understanding and dealing with what it symbolizes.

One final point about defining interculturality, which will be used as a red thread throughout the Element: the importance of language. In English, interculturality and its companions are already very diverse semantically. When one adds other languages, the complexity is staggering. In some languages the idea of interculturality is not even available (e.g. Chinese and Finnish), while in others one needs to play around to translate both *inter-* and *-ality*. In some languages, such as Spanish in South America, the word *interculturalidad* exists but it has very specific connotations and often relates to Indigenous groups. This is something that we also need to be curious about and reflecting on the (mis-)translation of terms matters as much as trying to find a clear definition of interculturality in 'one sentence'.

The Element thus urges us to be curious about other ways of defining, understanding and delimiting interculturality, not in order to restrict it but to help us open up to other ways of thinking about it so we may enrich ourselves as educators. Enclosing ourselves in a given monolingual and ideological cocoon of interculturality could easily go against the very idea of interculturality. I argue that teachers could deal with issues of interculturality more effectively if they could take the time and had the opportunity to reflect on and make sense of how others (students, colleagues, parents, decision makers) view the notion ideologically.

Why Should Interculturality Matter for Teachers, Teacher Educators and Scholars?

This subsection serves to continue justifying the importance of 'caring about' interculturality as educators. To me, the question goes hand in hand with another question: *why do we educate people?* As we have seen, what interculturality means and entails can be multiform in different contexts, languages and for different people. What is more, I have mentioned the fact that some of its companions (e.g. *multicultural* but also *cross-cultural, transcultural* or even *social justice*) can refer to similar realities or different ones, depending on the key terms used, foci and ideological backgrounds. I have also insisted on the polysemic use of the concept of *diversity*, which often appears alongside interculturality, referring to different entities. What could be similar in many perspectives relating to the notion in education is that they deal with the co-presence of people who are perceived to share both similarities and differences in, for example, a classroom setting; people might speak the same language (with variations) and/or share other (local, international) languages, and have come together to co-construct new knowledge together, having to negotiate and agree and disagree over it. Those involved might have the same passport or different passports; they might or might not have been born in the same town/city/village or country; they might or might not share the same political, economic and ideological perspectives and their economic-symbolic power statuses might differ (amongst others). We return here to the argument that teaching (and learning) is always intercultural *nolens volens*.

As mentioned previously, schools are directly impacted by world news and current domestic or global events and this has been more evident than before since January 2020, with major world crises hitting us. For example, when the war started in Ukraine in early 2022, funds were swiftly made available for promoting *peace education* and *education for emergencies* in both teacher education and training (professional development) in Finland. The ongoing crises of 2020–2 (I was writing this Element at the end of spring 2022) all had to do with interculturality, in the way we have dealt with the Covid-19 virus interculturally; the internationalization of the Black Lives Matter movement; the crisis of Afghanistan; again, the war in Ukraine and the international media literacy that one had to acquire to make sense of what was happening. Previous crises, such as the humanitarian crisis of 2016 following a five-year civil war in Syria, also had a direct 'intercultural' impact on the work of teachers in certain parts of the world.

Many initiatives have emerged over the past ten years to help teachers and teacher educators deal with aspects of interculturality for education. I note that they were not always placed under the label of interculturality. Many supra-national institutions have been active in promoting projects related to the topic. I present briefly two examples in what follows (focusing on supranational institutions that are both located in Europe).

The Organisation for Economic Co-operation and Development (OECD) launched a project called 'Teacher Education for Diversity' in 2010, which is described as follows:

> A key argument is that schools can do better in building on the capital of all students and benefit from diversity as a driving source for enhancing learning. One way in which they can do this is to use the strength and flexibility of their teachers, but of course for this to be effective teachers need to be given appropriate support and training. Teacher education and training programs play a central role here in determining the kind of knowledge and skills that teachers develop. (OECD, 2010)

Again, the keywords here are *diversity* and *global* and yet they relate very much to interculturality. As a reminder, the OECD, based in Paris, aims to influence policymakers from around the world in terms of prosperity, equality, opportunity and wellbeing for all. In the quote above, the use of the words 'capital' and 'benefit from' ('building on the capital of all students and benefit from diversity') falls within the domain of economic discourses. Amongst their activities, they have identified experiences and examples of good teacher education and classroom practice and developed a 'toolkit' containing teaching and education strategies for interculturality. The OECD is the organization that runs the Programme for International Student Assessment (PISA) studies with students aged fifteen from around the world. It is noteworthy that one of the competences tested by the studies is called global competence.

The Council of Europe is another institution that has actively been involved in preparing teachers for interculturality. Although the word *intercultural* used to be omnipresent in the work and 'tools' produced by the supranational institution, it has focused on the ideology of *democratic culture* since 2016 instead. *A Reference Framework of Competences for Democratic Culture* appeared in 2018, which presents twenty competences to be developed in students 'to prepare them for lives as active citizens in democratic societies' (Council of Europe, 2018). The reference framework revolves mostly around the work of British scholar Michael Byram (e.g. 1997) from language education and is anchored within the values of *citizenship*, *human rights*, *justice* and *politics*. The notion of the intercultural appears from time to time in the documents from the project but it does not assume a central place. In 2022, the Council of Europe published a document entitled the *Reference Framework of Competences for Democratic Culture: Teacher Reflection Tool*. The tool is meant to support teachers in their discovery of the reference framework and to self-reflect on teaching and democratic competences.

As far as teacher education and training are concerned, many programmes related to interculturality have been identified in some parts of the world. As such, in some countries, international bachelor's or master's programmes focus specifically on interculturality (or its companions) in education, many with a clear link to teacher education, while other 'mainstream' teacher education programmes contain some credits related to issues of diversity. Let me mention four examples. In Europe, Trinity College Dublin offers a master's in Education Studies, Intercultural Learning and Leadership. The programme aims are described as follows: 'to equip participants with the threshold academic knowledge of educational leadership, in the context of critical examination of race, language diversity, and religious diversity' (mie.ie, 2022). At the University of Oulu (Finland), a bachelor's programme entitled Intercultural Teacher Education (primary level) is available, with a three-month study or work period in an educational institution or a project abroad. Its content is described as 'built on cutting edge research and diverse teaching and learning methods and also considers the diversity of individual learners' (oulu.fi, 2022). The University of Houston (United States) has a master's in Multicultural Studies in Education, which is described as '[preparing] teachers to address equity and diversity issues within the class-room, school and the community while the Social Justice in Education focus offers a slightly broader focus, preparing educators and other professionals to explore, identify and advocate for human rights in a variety of environments, organizations and communities' (University of Houston, 2022). Finally, at the University of Nevada (United States), a master's in Equity and Diversity in Education aims to prepare teachers to 'work more effectively with individuals from various backgrounds'. They add: 'Multiple dimensions of human diversity are addressed through the program's course work, with special attention to gender, race/ethnicity, national origin, language, social class and exceptionality' (University of Nevada, 2022). From these four programmes, one can already get a sense of the diverse ways of engaging with interculturality as well as the influence of local ideologies on the way that interculturality is positioned within teacher education.

It is not my objective here to give an exhaustive overview of the thousands of political and educational initiatives to promote interculturality for teacher education. I do encourage you to be curious about the ones taking place in your context (looking into interculturality *and* its companions), as well as internationally. Stating the obvious but from the short presentation of initiatives and looking at today's world, interculturality does matter and is central to the work of educators and scholars in teacher education. To finish with the question of why interculturality matters, let us remember that interculturality 'flows' in many and varied aspects in the work of the teachers:

- *How to communicate* in class with each individual and groups, as well as outside class with, for example, colleagues and parents;
- *How to teach* – taking into account some of the aspects listed above – and what to teach (for example, trying to include knowledge from different parts of the globe);
- *How to prepare students to communicate* in class, in school and outside the school context for today and tomorrow;
- *How to (accept to) unlearn* how one sees the world, self and other to transform teaching and learning;
- *How to give a chance to all* in the classroom and beyond, to 'shine'.

Working with This Element

With this introduction we can already see that the 'world' of interculturality for teacher education is quite full and, maybe, somewhat confusing. One might be wondering if one can write anything that has not been 'chewed on' yet on the topic.

This Element is special because it will help us make sense of how people have engaged with interculturality for teacher education and reflect on how we might want to work with it ourselves. The Element especially aims at creating curiosity in the ways others see and use interculturality and helping us discard our fear of change that we might associate with the notion. Finally, the Element also urges us to be interested in the way we frame 'things' for interculturality in different languages so that we can enrich our own thinking in teacher education.

The following sections were written somewhat differently, and are meant to serve different purposes by dialoguing in-/directly with each other. While Section 2 offers an extensive discussion of a literature review, Section 3 (which draws conclusions from Section 2) supports us in engaging critically and reflexively with interculturality. In constructing these sections, I followed the reflexive and critical perspective that I have employed with pre-service and in-service teachers in Finland. Section 2 reviews some of the recent international literature on issues of interculturality for teacher education and identifies the main research results which can inspire us to unthink and rethink interculturality as an object of research and education. At the same time, Section 2 helps us practise reflexivity and criticality in the way international research frames and deals with interculturality in teacher education. In this section, we mostly listen to researchers from selected parts of the world and start thinking about how we see their research results and the ideologies they might contain. Section 3 problematizes interculturality for teacher education *otherwise*. This section is written in a more creative manner in the sense that it is devised in a way that would support you in your own reflexive and critical engagement with the notion. In the section we learn to take into account contextual and linguistic discussions of interculturality and to make informed choices about the way we problematize, discuss and put interculturality into practice in our teaching and research. In the final section in the Element, I come back to the central ideas of reflexivity and criticality in interculturality for teacher education and summarize the main points made in the sections, guiding you to 'piece together' the jigsaw of interculturality in teacher education.

In order to boost the critical and reflexive experience of reading this Element, I have included reflexive questions for you to consider before reading each section ('Reflect Before Reading the Section') and at the end ('Thinking Further').

I hope that you will enjoy reading the Element and that it will help you make sense of some of the complexities of interculturality as an object of research and education *for yourself*. It is not a recipe book and, again, it will not teach you how to 'do' interculturality. I wrote this Element to tell (pre-service and in-service) teachers, teacher educators and scholars from different contexts that there is 'diversity' out there in the way we see and 'do' interculturality in the world, and that our role as educators should be to be excited by all this complexity and eager to move forward together.

Thinking Further

- What is the most important element that you have already learnt about interculturality as an object of research and education in the introduction to this Element?
- What is it that you are looking forward to the most in the following sections? Why? How do you think these might help you in your own practice and/or research?
- Are you disappointed that the author does not directly define interculturality in the introduction? After consulting some of his previous publications, are you able to explain how he would probably define the notion? How different and similar does his take appear to be compared to yours?
- Are you aware of any national or international projects related to interculturality (and its companions) for teacher education and training? What do you know about them? Have you yourself been on a course or part of a project?
- What does the word *diversity* mean in your context, especially in education? Who does it include/exclude?
- How much do you know about the conceptual companions of interculturality such as *cross-cultural*, *multicultural*, *transcultural* and/or *global*? Do you know how to define them? Are you aware of any scholars who have written about these concepts/notions?

2 Interculturality for Teacher Education: The Simplexity of Previous Research

Objectives

- To review some of the international literature on issues of interculturality for teacher education;
- To identify the main research results which can inspire us to unthink and rethink interculturality as an object of research and education;
- To practise reflexivity and criticality in relation to how international research frames and deals with interculturality in teacher education;

- To prepare for Section 3, where we will problematize interculturality for teacher education *otherwise*.

Reflect Before Reading the Section

- What research have you read about interculturality for teacher education? In what language(s) and from which parts of the world? Which concepts and notions were used in the publications to discuss what it is about and how it functions in education?
- Who wrote these publications? Where are they from? What is their take on interculturality? How do they define it and describe the way it could be tackled in teacher education – for example, do they put forward 'models of intercultural competence'?
- How much has the literature you have consulted helped you concretely in your work as a teacher?
- Do you have a clear idea of what topics have been researched in relation to interculturality in teacher education?
- What paradigms and ideologies seem to dominate teacher education in your institutional and national contexts? What kinds of policies?
- Finally, reflect on the meaning(s) of the following keywords in English and other languages, globally and in your own context (in alphabetical order): *citizenship, competence, critical, equity/equality, social justice*. These are some of the polysemic words that we are going to introduce in this section and I would like you to reflect on their meanings and connotations. I suggest that you do the same exercise every time you come across a word related to interculturality for teacher education that might look 'obvious' in the section.

A First Look at the *Bric-a-Brac* of Terms and Ideas

Bric-a-brac refers to a miscellaneous collection of small articles and curiosities. Although the term might sound 'negative' to some of us, it is not used in a pejorative way here. It is a reminder of the need to think beyond the box of what the very word interculturality might mean to us.

This section takes us through the 'maze' of (some of the) international research on interculturality for teacher education. I use the portmanteau word of *simplexity*, composed of *simplicity* and *complexity*, to describe the literature I introduce: it will appear simple and complex, as well as complex and simple at the same time. These are the questions I am asking: *what does previous research tell us about the topic? What can we learn from it? How can we use it critically and reflexively in our work as educators?* At the same time, I am interested in supporting you in reflecting on what we can learn from *how* research reports results about interculturality for teacher education: *what problems can we identify in research itself? What seems to be missing from it?* The elements collected here are derived from publications published between 2017 and 2022 in English only, since this is the main source that I assume all readers will have access to. However, it is important to consult literature published in different languages and in one's own context(s). We need to beware of treating localized teacher education through (imported) politically and ideologically influenced perspectives without looking at them critically and reflexively. Section 3 will help us reflect on this aspect.

In order to write Section 2, I combed through research articles in various research databases, using different keywords such as *intercultural/multicultural teacher education, culturally responsive teacher education* and *global teacher education*. As mentioned in the introduction, I could have also focused on, for example, inclusive education and language and intercultural education for teachers (two fields that have contributed in their own ways to intercultural scholarship); however, I decided to start with broader research labels for my review directly connected to teacher education. The two fields will appear here and there in the section.

I started by identifying review papers on the topics represented by the keywords. In total I collected around fifty articles from 2017–22. In this section I will be referring to approximately thirty of them, having left aside some of the articles because of the minor contributions they were making to new knowledge about interculturality for teacher education. My goal is not to present an exhaustive picture of the very complex field of interculturality for teacher education but to share some insights into it to both prepare ourselves for Section 3 and to trigger some curiosity in you. Acquainting ourselves with the international literature related to interculturality for teacher education is, at first, extremely overwhelming since there are so many publications in English, with an increasing number working towards more 'critical' approaches to interculturality. This is a good thing as it shows that the topic is taken seriously in teacher education. Yet, one notices that the international literature only covers some parts of the world empirically and even fewer theoretically and conceptually. For example, in a systematic review of multicultural education research published internationally in recent years, Uzunboylu and Altay (2021) show that scholars from forty-eight countries have produced research on the topic. The following countries produced most of the studies: the United States, followed by Turkey, Finland, the Republic of Korea, Australia, Canada and the United Kingdom. Countries with clearly fewer papers included, for example, China, Malaysia, South Africa, and marginally, Kazakhstan, Sweden, Chile, Ethiopia, Indonesia and Jordan. At first sight, one can consider the knowledge produced to be 'diverse' since it emerges from

the whole world. Yet, as we shall see later, the ideological and scientific positioning appears to be very much Western-centric when it comes to teacher education,
such as in the way the objectives and practices of interculturality are put into
words. As such, at a recent PhD defence in English about multicultural (teacher)
education in the Nordics, where the student was Nordic and the opponent an
American scholar, one could see how the American ideological sphere of 'critical
multicultural education' was dominating and pushing the candidate to speak in
ways that seemed to make them repeat certain US-centric 'critical' ideologies,
somewhat uncritically.

Examining the literature published around interculturality in teacher education, one notices long lists of different terms – a *bric-a-brac* of terms and ideas –
used to refer to the act of taking 'diversity' into account. Table 1 provides us
with a snapshot of the phrases used to refer to the field in English from
publications from the period 2017–22 (in alphabetical order).

It is important to say here that many other labels are available in the global
literature that I have omitted here, labels that focus, for example, only on linguistic
diversity (e.g. multilingual teacher education). Many other constructs such as
education for democracy, peace education and *anti-racism education* are not
included in the discussion below because of space constraints. I note that these
labels are also relevant for what we are doing here and I would encourage readers to
explore them too. Although all of these are different labels, they all aim to prepare
teachers for dealing with diversity in schools. My goal here is not to present each

Table 1 List of terms identified in the literature to refer
to interculturality for teacher education.

- Critical multicultural education
- Culturally relevant pedagogy
- Culturally responsive teaching
- Culturally sustaining pedagogy
- Global teacher education
- Intercultural teacher training
- Interculturality and teacher education
- Linguistically responsive teaching
- Multicultural and social justice teacher education
- Multicultural teacher education
- Social justice education
- Sustainable intercultural and inclusive education
- Teaching for diversity
- Transformative teacher education for diverse
  students

and every one of these perspectives. Theoretically, ideologically and economic-politically they might differ, overlap and be diverse *from within*. We note that different terms are used in these labels, with some related to *culture*, others with more 'social activist' connotations (*social justice*, *critical*), and one which has to do with *language*. As a reminder, this list is not exhaustive in English and if we extend our research to other contexts and languages it would become even more complex. One will find an uncountable number of different labels on the 'market'. I argue that there is no need to panic about this complexity at this stage.

A few more introductory comments are provided here: most of the labels emerged within the context of North America and have been adopted and somewhat adapted elsewhere. I present specificities of some of these perspectives below, bearing in mind that the way these are discussed in the articles might not be shared by all scholars using them around the world.

- The notions of *intercultural* and *multicultural* are often found alongside *teacher education*, and although we are told that the *inter-* and *multi-* connote differently – for example, *inter-* is more dynamic, it is about processes; multicultural is more 'patchwork-like' and static, see Abdallah-Pretceille, 1999 – they cannot be dichotomized so easily since many researchers seem to use the terms interchangeably. Their use is clearly influenced by geopolitical locations too. Both emerged from the 'West', with narratives about their origins describing *multicultural* as being 'American' (civil rights movements of the 1960s) and *intercultural* more 'European' (decolonization period from the 1970s onwards). According to Lash et al. (2022: 121): 'Multiculturalism tends to focus on cultural awareness and antibias practices, whereas interculturalism focuses on open-mindedness, an awareness of others, and a willingness and ability to interact effectively with those different from oneself, which is more behaviorally focused.' Such somewhat simplistic boundary-making between the two notions deserves to be questioned – not every scholar we engage with agrees. In Finland, for example, where none of these constructs dominate politically, scholars and educators might navigate between them, without necessarily differentiating them, or defining them in ways that would not be considered as stable (see Holm & Zilliacus, 2009; Dervin & Tournebise, 2013). There are also differences in the way they are used in the three majority languages in this Nordic country: English, Finnish and Swedish.
- Adding 'critical' to the two previous notions, some scholars have wanted to make a difference with perspectives that they refer to pejoratively as 'liberal' (in the case of multicultural education) and/or 'essentialist' (for (language and) intercultural education). *Critical* often refers to discussions of power relations, inequalities, social injustice and othering in intercultural/multicultural education

(e.g. Gorski, 2009; Holliday, 2010). Nieto and Bode (2018: 40) interpret *critical* in these labels as 'education for social justice', another perspective from the US context that is found in the list above. Some of the critical perspectives might also be based on, for example, postmodern, posthuman and decolonizing and/or critical race theory (see the last subsection of this section). These perspectives, with political and ideological grounding in the United States, are increasingly found in educational research in the European context and beyond.

• *Culturally responsive teaching* was proposed by American scholar Gay (2010: 31) and defined as 'using the cultural knowledge, prior experiences, frames of reference, and performance styles of ethnically diverse students to make learning encounters more relevant to and effective for them'. The assumption is that when students learn and can connect knowledge to, for example, their own cultural background, the process of learning is more meaningful and richer. The keywords here are 'ethnic' and 'culture', which are polysemic in English and other languages, potentially leading to confusion in scholars and teachers around the world. There is also a danger of labelling and treating students according to how one sees them as 'representatives' of 'cultures' and different 'ethnic groups' – on critiques of the concept of culture, see, for example, Wikan (2002). For example, in a Finnish classroom, I witnessed an episode where a white female teacher asked a black female student to talk about the kinds of fruit eaten in the 'African culture' – a request to which the student replied that she had no idea since she had never been to Africa and only spoke Finnish and was a Finnish citizen, before shedding tears of frustration.

• Although the label of *global* is not widespread (yet) in naming a kind of interculturality for teacher education, it has been identified in the literature. For example, Pais and Costa (2020) show how the label seems to correspond to 'critical democracy', with ethical values, social responsibility and active citizenry at its core, in reaction to global neoliberalism, privileging a market rationale focused on self-investment and enhanced profits. We shall come back to the label of *global* later on in the section.

Beyond the many and varied terms used to describe the different forms of teacher education associated with interculturality, it is also of interest to note that the expected outcomes or the kinds of skills/competences that teachers should develop for dealing with interculturality and diversity are manifold in the litera-ture. In Table 2 I list the phrases used for these elements and recurrent models and frameworks found in the recent literature (in alphabetical order again).

Here again we have a sample of the diversity of expected outcomes, with similar words being used, for example, *cultural* (as well as *cross-cultural*, *intercultural* and *multicultural*) and *global*. A variety of terms are used for the

Table 2 Labels for the kinds of skills/competences expected from teachers and models.

- Cross-cultural skills
- Cultural intelligence
- Cultural understanding
- Dispositions for global education
- Diversity consciousness/awareness
- Global citizenship
- Global competence
- Global mindsets
- Intercultural awareness
- Intercultural competence
- Intercultural integration
- Intercultural sensitivities
- Intercultural understanding
- Multicultural dispositions
- Multicultural teaching efficacy
- Development Model of Intercultural Sensitivity (Bennett, 2004)
- Framework of Cultural Competence (Sue & Sue, 2013)
- Intercultural Development Continuum (Hammer, 2009)
- Model of Intercultural Communicative Competence (Byram, 1997)
- Model of Sources of Cultural Identity (Cushner et al., 2006)
- Multicultural Teacher Dispositions Scale (Jensen et al., 2016)

expected outcomes: *awareness, citizenship, competence, consciousness, dispositions, efficacy, integration, intelligence, sensitivities, skills, understanding*. Each of them connotes different (educational, psychological, political) aspects and can be misleading when and if used in different languages (e.g. how should *integration* or *citizenship* be translated in other languages?). I note that only one of these terms has to do explicitly with teaching: *multicultural teaching efficacy*.

In terms of the tools used for either developing or assessing the skills considered to be necessary, six have been identified in the consulted literature, all from either the UK or the United States. There are three *models*, one *continuum*, one *framework* and a *scale*. Some use the idea of *competence*, others *identity* or *dispositions*.

Finally, before reviewing some of the aforementioned terms, we note that some share similar assumptions and characteristics while differing ideologically and in terms of paradigms. A few words about three of these terms are shared in what follows.

The idea of *intercultural competence* (sometimes found in the plural or spelt as *competencies*) has been in use for several decades in different subfields of research on intercultural communication education. It has also been promoted by supranational institutions (see Spitzberg & Changnon, 2009; Dervin et al., 2020). Some models of intercultural competence have dominated the broad field of intercultural communication education for decades, such as Byram's (1997) Intercultural Communicative Competence model from foreign language education (UK); Deardorff's (2006) model for internationalization and higher education (United States) and Bennett's (2004) Developmental Model of Intercultural Sensitivity within the field of communication. These have long been used beyond their original fields and are commonly referred to in the international literature on teacher education. Byram's work has long been associated with that of a supranational political institution called the Council of Europe, which aims to promote values such as 'Democracy' and 'Human Rights', and throughout his work, the political stances of the Council have dominated his scholarship. For example, in his recent publications, *competence* seems to have been reframed and replaced by *citizenship* (Porto et al., 2018), and in his work for the Council of Europe, *intercultural* by *democratic culture* (Council of Europe, 2018). His model includes elements such as *knowledge of self and other*, *knowledge of interaction* and *relativising self-valuing other*. Deardorff's (2006) model is based on Delphi studies on existing Western models, which she synthesized and combined into a 'new' model composed of *attitude, knowledge, skills, internal outcomes* and *external outcomes*. In 2021, the United Nations Educational, Scientific and Cultural Organization (UNESCO) published her *Manual for Developing Intercultural Competencies* open access with Routledge, around the idea of Study Circles. I note that the OECD's (2018) model of global competence (OECD, 2018a) is based on Deardorff's model too. Bennett (2004) has used the construct of intercultural sensitivity as some kind of synonym for intercultural competence. His take on the idea is that one can progress through one's intercultural sensitivity, reaching levels of better 'quality'. The assumptions behind all these models differ somehow but they also share similarities, such as in their use of the polysemic concept of *culture*, which they rarely problematize or modify, and in the fact that their 'models' were created solely through the English language in the Western hemisphere, which indirectly or directly imposes specific ideologies. Finally, I note that there have been attempts at assessing such competences in teachers, which have not proven to be too successful (e.g. Thapa, 2020) – see the subsection on assessment in this section.

The concept of *global* is increasingly used to describe what is expected of teachers interculturally. For example, Tambyah (2019: 108) defines *dispositions for global education* as 'increased knowledge of cultures, acknowledging and addressing stereotypes and personal growth in accepting oneself and others'. In an article on the global mindsets of teachers, Goodwin (2020) proposes taking into account the impact of globalization on teachers by introducing four dimensions for teachers and teacher educators, asking how teachers could interrupt and resist its negative impacts on classrooms and learners. The four dimensions (Goodwin, 2020: 11–14) include: *the curricular* (content, histories and perspectives beyond local and national boundaries, from the perspective of global citizenry; asking questions such as 'what knowledge is of most worth?', 'who has the power to decide worthwhile knowledge?', 'what values, beliefs and ways of knowing are privileged?'; 'how do we come to know ourselves?'); *the professional* (teachers around the world recognize that they are part of a global community of about 80 million teachers and celebrate their spirit from a global perspective – 'collective agency'); *the moral* (recentring their work on humanity, social action and caring about tackling world problems); and *the personal* (self-reflection, interrogation and evaluation, questioning our values, beliefs, biases, expectations and tacit knowledge . . . in confrontation with the 'Other').

Finally, let me introduce briefly the idea of *multicultural teaching efficacy,* which is defined by Guyton and Wesche (2005: 23) as teachers' confidence in how well they can teach students from culturally diverse backgrounds in multicultural classrooms. Teacher efficacy is a concept that has been amply researched and there seems to be an assumption in the global literature that efficacy leads to 'good' teaching practices and rapport. For example, Fitchett et al. (2012) show that teachers exposed to multicultural education perspectives such as culturally responsive teaching are empowered to be more inclusive in the way they treat diverse students.

I hope that the first snapshots of the simplexities around research on interculturality in and for teacher education in international publications in English will not have discouraged the reader. What I wanted to do was to show that getting into the topic is not easy because of the multitude of terms and perspectives. I am often asked which term one should use to talk about interculturality for teacher education and what differences there might be between them. At this stage I would say that these questions – although 'normal' since, I repeat, the simplexities are a bit overwhelming – are not so important. As we have seen, to date there has been an uncountable list of terms with different and sometimes overlapping ideologies, objectives and discourses. Choosing and combining them can be based on personal choices. What matters, as we shall see, is that we know why we choose specific terms, models and frameworks, and are aware of the potential consequences of these choices on our own beliefs, practices and actions as educators and scholars.

Overview of Research Topics

Policies and Research Reviews

To continue our exploration of interculturality for teacher education, we now focus on two recent reviews of policies and research (for earlier reviews see, for example, Cochran-Smith & Villegas, 2015). These serve the purpose of illustrating the diversity of studies available, to give a sense of the 'flavours' given to the topic in global research. Yet they do not aim to generalize about how this is dealt with in glocalized contexts, that is, in local contexts embedded in the global, and in different languages. The studies are presented following a chronological order.

Let us start with a paper from my own context. In 'Diverging discourses on multicultural education in Finnish teacher education programme policies: Implications for teaching', Hummelstedt-Djedou et al. (2018) investigate the kind of discourses on multicultural education found in Finnish teacher education policies. On the basis of the key terms of *multicultural(ism)*, *intercultural(ity)*, *social justice*, *equality* and *equity*, and following an American scholar's tripartite model of *conservative*, *liberal* and *critical multiculturalism*, the authors note that what they identified in teacher education policies reflects mostly *conservative approaches* ('facts' about diversity, mostly about immigrants, presenting them as a problem), with very few *'critical' perspectives* (*critical* seems to mean engaging with 'social justice', i.e. fighting against 'inequalities'). Different Finnish universities seemed to have different perspectives, with only a few adopting 'critical' ones. As a conclusion, the authors claim that 'student teachers from different teacher education programmes become unequally competent in teaching for social justice' (Hummelstedt-Djedou et al., 2018: 197). They add: 'we would like to call attention to the other aims of multicultural education, such as seeing everybody as part of diversity, taking diversity into account, analysing structures and our own privileges critically, and changing society towards equality' (Hummelstedt-Djedou et al., 2018: 198). The insistence on issues of social justice, equity and equality will be found in many perspectives on interculturality for teacher education. I note at this stage that the idea of social justice, for example, is rarely articulated concretely. As such what it refers to appears to be fuzzy and issues of equal access to/fair distribution of capital, 'money', for example, are never named directly, although they do matter. Social justice appears to be a synonym for discourses of anti-discrimination, anti-racism and epistemic justice, for example. I do not diminish their importance here but I wonder if and how social justice can be dealt with if economic discussions do not take place openly. Finally, and this comment will often reappear in what follows: although the study under review looks at the Finnish context – which has its own specific discourses and entries into issues of diversity and interculturality – the conceptual 'gauges' are mostly derived from the United States.

In 'How does initial teacher education research frame the challenge of preparing future teachers for student diversity in schools? A systematic review of literature', Rowan et al. (2021) insist on the importance of knowing more about teacher educators' knowledge base on interculturality for teacher education. As such, teacher educators have a central role to play in preparing teachers for dealing with diversity in their future careers. The decisions they make about the kind of knowledge to share have an impact on pre-service teachers' future job. The authors first discuss the factors constraining teacher educators in preparing teachers: *contextual constraints* (e.g. policies, politics and institutions; neoliberal, conservative political environments); *challenges linked to pre-service teachers* (e.g. beliefs in their ability to work with diverse students); and *challenges to learning linked to teacher educators* (e.g. how their own beliefs shape what they teach about interculturality, their confidence in preparing future teachers for diverse learners). In the paper Rowan et al. (2021: 135) also present claims made about how teacher education can prepare future teachers for diverse learners in terms of the aims and content of courses and programmes:

1. By asserting the existence of a knowledge base *about* diversity (largely concentrating on demographic/population facts and the ways these groups have been historically at risk of educational alienation or failure) that future teachers need to possess
2. By outlining frameworks, pedagogies and practices associated with *catering to* these identified forms of diversity that future teachers need to be able to display
3. By highlighting the broader sociocritical and sociopolitical affordances of teacher education in relation to interrogating, problematizing, and reimagining diversity *for* social justice.

To summarize: *teachers need knowledge about facts about various forms of diversity* (e.g. 'at-risk group of learners' such as Latino children in the United States, migrants in Finland or students with disabilities in Korea); *teachers need to be able to use this knowledge in order to 'cater to diversity'* (e.g. making use of specific teacher practices, critical self-reflection, participatory action research, using culturally relevant pedagogy, development of socio-emotional skills); *teachers need to be supported in teaching for diversity through more politicized and critical theories, moving beyond mere 'facts' and 'catering'* (e.g. making use of specific theoretical perspectives related to categories of diversity, use of postcolonial theory and critical race theory to analyse race in education with an aim to lead to educational transformation).

Based on their review of the literature, the authors draw three important conclusions: 1. The approaches are many and varied, with some being more dynamic than others, wishing to disrupt authentically the system by teaching *for* diversity, rather than merely *about* or *to*. The latter have been referred to as the 'recognition/celebration' approaches, and have been deemed inadequate to trigger change in both teachers and the system. However, they seem to dominate the papers reviewed by the authors (Rowan et al., 2021). 2. Teacher educators need not be naïve about the illusion that there is a 'one-size-fits-all tool kit' of strategies leading to more active and transformative actions. Preparing teachers to analyse and act theoretically and politically in various contexts appears to be the most viable strategy. All in all, Rowan et al. (2021) recommend that teacher educators wishing to engage their students with interculturality and diversity should demonstrate what they call 'critical epistemic reflexivity', that is, a diversity of ways of knowing and doing, to develop teacher education *for* diversity (rather than just *about* or *to*).

This first entry into the literature, based on a selection of studies, shows that the theoretical, conceptual and political backbone (e.g. policies and previous research) is based on multiple perspectives, with some considered better and more appropriate than others. This first review subsection also provides us with a general idea of the kinds of hindrances that teacher educators face in specific contexts. We can also already sense a strong push towards more active and socially just approaches for teacher education.

Teachers' Assumptions, Beliefs, Experiences and Practices

A large number of English-language papers that I have identified focus on pre-service and in-service teachers' beliefs and practices. As most review papers on teacher multicultural/intercultural education note, the topic is popular. Already in the early 2010s, Castro (2010) had shown that two decades of literature on pre-service teachers' beliefs about multicultural education emphasized teachers' simplistic grasp of multicultural issues. A lack of research on the topic with in-service teachers was also already noted. *How do teachers view interculturality? How much do they seem to care about it? And what do they claim they do with it?*

In what follows I present studies from different parts of the world (China, The Netherlands, Turkey, the United States and the UK) concerning elementary teachers' and pre-service teachers' (with or without international experience) beliefs and perceptions about diversity. The review is chronological.

Cherng and Davis published a paper in 2017 based on the analysis of a large dataset of pre-service teachers' beliefs and student teacher performance assessments in the United States. They note that some diverse student teachers (e.g. Latinos but not Asian Americans – individuals are categorized in terms of 'race' in the paper since it is ideologically embedded in the US context) report more awareness and sensitivity of multicultural issues than their white counterparts. Having worked with non-dominant individuals is also seen as leading to higher levels of awareness in pre-service teacher education. Finally, the authors maintain that pre-service teachers in a wide range of content areas claim different levels of multicultural awareness; for example, pre-service early childhood teachers report higher levels than mathematics pre-service teachers. According to the authors, the results can inform teacher education policies by targeting pre-service teachers who need more input concerning interculturality than others.

Aragona-Young and Sawyer's (2018) article deals with elementary teachers' beliefs about multicultural education practices in the United States. They note problems with teachers being unable to define *culture* precisely and the low commitment they make to multicultural practices. They remind us, rightly, that working from beliefs and discourses may not reveal the complexities of how teachers engage concretely with diversity in classrooms and that their *real* practices might be more versatile depending on, for example, the context and access to resources. In a 2021 paper based on an international school in the Netherlands, the results of Roiha and Sommier (2021) differ somewhat from the previous study. Although in-service teachers all reported caring for and 'doing' intercultural education, their discourses on interculturality and diversity were limited to national cultures and traditions in class, with a few of them opening up to more critical views on interculturality beyond mere catalogues of culturalist perspectives, that is, solid and often stereotypical representations of national cultures (see Holliday, 2010).

In Yuan's (2018) paper about educating culturally responsive Han-Minzu ('ethnic') majority teachers working with Minzu minorities in Mainland China, we can read that, based on semi-structured interviews and focus groups with five pre-service K-12 teachers in Beijing, the pre-service teachers explained that they felt that students from other Minzu groups had *no culture* and only referred to the dichotomy of 'Chinese culture' versus 'Western culture' when they were prompted about multiculturalism and diversity in China. The teachers also insisted on the fact that such notions had been imported from the United States and were not useful for working with Minzu minority students. I note here again that the theoretical and conceptual perspectives are directly borrowed from the US intellectual sphere, which could easily influence the results of the study by creating a potential 'clash of ideologies'. As such, China has very specific ways of discussing and dealing with Minzu 'minority' education, placing at the centre issues of *diversity and unity, economic development* and *equality* (Dervin & Yuan, 2021). Trying to 'paper-trace' multicultural education research from a context where issues of diversity and interculturality differ immensely might blind us in examining the work, beliefs and actions of teachers if they are not used critically and reflexively.

The three following papers focus on the potential transformative power of further training and/or experience on beliefs and perceptions of interculturality in the work of the teacher.

In 'Challenging beliefs about cultural diversity in education: A synthesis and critical review of trainings with pre-service teachers', Civitillo et al. (2019) explain that most trainings concerning diversity in education attempt to address beliefs towards diverse students and their families. Many of the reviewed studies highlight the good effects of the trainings on pre-service teachers' beliefs about cultural diversity. However, the authors note that factors such as incoherence and contradictions hidden behind beliefs concerning cultural diversity are rarely discussed during the trainings reviewed. Although they also highlight limitations in, for example, study designs and training evaluations, which can hinder the validity of the trainings, the reviewed papers underline that experiential learning is a good option for modifying pre-service teachers' beliefs.

The last two studies of this subsection focus on the influence of two initiatives found in different educational contexts: previous intercultural experiences and 'diversity weeks'. Beutel and Tangen's (2018) paper suggests that pre-service teachers with intercultural experiences can learn to use this 'fund' to help them understand and work with diverse learners. Using Hammer's (2009) Intercultural Development Continuum, they show that prior quality engagement in interculturality does enhance pre-service teachers' intercultural competence and thus opportunities for working successfully in diverse educational contexts.

Finally, Puttick et al. (2021) identify shifts in pre-service teachers' perceptions about aspects such as gender, race and sexuality after a 'diversity week' in the UK. For example, after visiting a school in another (more diverse) area, pre-service teachers reported feeling more confident to teach Black, Asian and Minority Ethnic students. The authors suggest that, in order to enrich such initiatives, further active and critical discussions around whiteness and structural inequalities should be systematized.

This subsection has highlighted the importance of reflecting on one's assumptions and beliefs on interculturality and our abilities to deal with them in the work of teachers. There appear to be similarities in the ways teachers discuss these issues in the aforementioned studies. What the authors often note is the impossibility to find out if beliefs and assumptions can be 'reverted' or 'corrected'. This is not surprising as such since actions do not always correspond to discourses and assertions. One might claim to have 'no stereotypes' about a certain group of people, before uttering an essentializing comment about the same group and acting in a discriminatory manner. These contradictions must thus be reflected on and strategies must be conceptualized and 'practised' to be able to move one step further in bridging the gaps they represent. Criticality and reflexivity, which will be discussed in length in Section 3, represent interesting options in this regard.

Developing and Assessing Intercultural Competence in Teacher Education

This topic looks deeper into the competences expected from (future) teachers in relation to interculturality and diversity. As already mentioned, different constructs have been used in the papers that I consulted to name expected outcomes: *cultural competence, multicultural competence, intercultural competence, intercultural sensitivity* and *multicultural dispositions* (amongst others). The following studies have taken place in different parts of the world, such as Bosnia and Herzegovina, Georgia, Indonesia, Serbia and the United States.

In all the papers one feels a dedication towards infusing reflections on developing specific competences for interculturality in teacher education. While some papers describe some advancement in both problematizing and attempting to implement strategies for developing such competences, other papers admit that very little is done in teacher education to make a difference. This is the case of Beljanski and Dedić Bukvić's (2020) paper about teacher education in Serbia, Bosnia and Herzegovina, where they find that curricula to develop the intercultural competences of pre-service teachers are nearly nonexistent. Many institutions around the world do not systematically include these issues in their curricula either.

In 'Delphi investigation of strategies to develop cultural competence in physical education teacher education', Wyant et al. (2020) examine how physical education teacher education programmes try to support the development of cultural competence amongst pre-service teachers. A series of strategies to promote cultural competence were negotiated between the study participants who were teacher educators from the United States and other countries: *critical awareness/cultural knowledge, skills development* (e.g. problem-solving, critical thinking), *organizational support* and *department commitment* (e.g. leaders' willingness to have a positive impact on structures; Wyant et al., 2020).

Although such strategies matter, what 'cultural competence' for teacher educators means is neither defined nor problematized in the article. The need to make issues such as race and social justice relevant is emphasized but appears to be treated in a broad and polysemic way.

In an article about pre-service teachers in multi-ethnic Indonesia, Solehuddin and Budiman (2019) identify existing multicultural competences of pre-service pre-school teachers and designed a training model to increase their multicultural awareness. Using Western elements – mostly American (e.g. Erickson Cornish et al., 2010) – to define multicultural competence, the following aspects are retained by the authors: 1. awareness and bias of their own values; 2. awareness and bias of others' (children's) culture; and 3. learning intervention strategy for culturally responsive teaching. Each element consists of the three following dimensions (often identified in models of intercultural/multicultural competence): attitudes and beliefs, knowledge, and skills.

The issue of assessment of competences with a focus on pre-service teachers has been identified in many publications. In Georgia, Tabatadze et al. (2020) used Bennett's (2004) Development Model of Intercultural Sensitivity and Cushner et al.'s (2006) model of sources of cultural identity for assessing the intercultural sensitivity of pre-service teachers. They showed that most of the teachers were in the 'ethnocentric phase', that is, they were unable to think beyond their own worldview in and about their teaching. They also found that few teachers were open to and tolerant of diversity. In 'Measuring the multicultural dispositions of preservice teachers', Jensen et al. (2016) in a study conducted in the United States define the kinds of dispositions required of future teachers and include *empathy, meekness (humility), social awareness, inclusion* and *advocacy*, on the basis of a literature review. Their article develops a new survey tool. One important finding is the confirmation that pre-service teachers might be experiencing some kind of 'Hawthorne effect', that is, when observed, they modify their responses, maybe to be more socially desirable, which might place doubt on the validity of using assessment instruments for interculturality for teacher education.

Table 3 summarizes the examples presented in this subsection. As we can see, different labels are used and they all seem to emerge from the US context, even in the studies about Georgia and Indonesia. Some elements contained in these 'models' overlap and differ, although they might be 'named' differently. How and why scholars and educators prefer certain labels over others can be explained by personal/scientific preferences, received training and access to knowledge (amongst others); however, they are rarely justified. What appears to be clear in the consulted papers is that confirming the validity of assessing such competences is difficult – if not impossible – especially over the long term.

Table 3 Types of competences for teacher education.

Reference	Population	Type of competence
Wyant et al. (2020) •	Teacher educators from the United States and a few other 'countries' (referred to as 'Asia, Asia-Pacific, Europe, Southeast Asia')	**Cultural competence** including *critical awareness/cultural knowledge, skills development, organizational support, department commitment.*
Solehuddin and Budiman (2019)	Pre-service pre-school teachers in Indonesia	**Multicultural competences** including *awareness and bias of their own values; awareness and bias of others' (children's) culture; learning intervention strategy for culturally responsive teaching*
Tabatadze et al. (2020)	Pre-service teachers in Georgia	**Intercultural sensitivity** based on *Bennett's (2004) Development Model of Intercultural Sensitivity* and *Cushner et al.'s (2006) model of sources of cultural identity*
Jensen et al. (2016)	Pre-service teachers in the United States	**Multicultural dispositions** including *empathy, meekness, social awareness, inclusion* and *advocacy*

Scholars like Zarate and Gohard-Radenkovic (2005) introduced this issue in the early 2000s and recommended talking about 'recognizing' that we all have these competences but that they are used 'unstably' rather than trying to assess them by means of measures that cannot grasp the complexity of 'doing' interculturality. The question of who decides on the elements to include in definitions of the types of competences to implement and 'assess' is a question that we also need to bear in mind all the time.

Professional Development and Teaching Initiatives

In the previous subsections, most of the reviewed literature dealt with pre-service teachers. In what follows, I examine professional development initiatives for both pre-service and in-service teachers in different parts of the world. The question asked here is: *how are teachers supported in relation to the intercultural?* Professional development includes here actions and activities aiming to support educators in improving student learning and social aspects of schooling (e.g. teacher–student intercultural relations). A large number of publications show that there is an increasing interest in trying to spread and improve interculturality for teacher education.

In the recent literature, two papers have proposed reviews of the literature on multicultural education professional development. We start with Parkhouse et al. (2019). Based on a review of forty studies of multicultural education–focused professional development programmes they identified important questions and considerations. These include (Parkhouse et al., 2019: 416):

- how PD [Professional Development] providers navigate tensions or challenges arising from resistance to discussions of diversity and equity;
- locating the balance between providing specific knowledge about students' cultures and guarding against promoting stereotypes or broad generalizations;
- researchers and PD developers should also pay close attention to their underlying theories related to both teacher learning and multicultural education.

The reviewed programmes were very different, although they all seemed to support teachers to reflect on, analyse and create instructional materials to make teaching more intercultural. Theoretically, the way issues of diversity were conceptualized differed in the professional development initiatives. Although American perspectives such as *culturally relevant pedagogy* dominated, the authors noted loose interpretations and inconsistencies in the way they were used and referred to. Teachers were asked to reflect on their identities, otherness and different kinds of -isms (sexism, racism, etc.). However, the important aspects of *equity* and *empowerment* were often relegated to second place compared to *inclusion* and *intercultural understanding*. Pedagogically, most of the programmes provided teachers with knowledge about, for example, groups of students (e.g. Latinx culture in the United States) but did not systematically propose strategies to deal with more specific issues. At the end of the paper, the authors suggest paying attention to the delivery of knowledge about specific groups so as not to provide teachers with too stereotypical views. Regarding the types of activities used for the programmes, many papers reported for instance making use of critical friendships through which teachers observed colleagues' lessons and engaged in feedback; using self-evaluation through rubric rating and video analysis; and having the opportunity to immerse themselves in other educational contexts or home visits. Parkhouse et al. (2019) also examine the duration and intensity of programmes reported in the literature they consulted and noted major differences, whereby some programmes lasted one day and others were spread over a period of five years. They note that the potential impact of duration is rarely addressed in the papers but that this might be an important element to look into. Finally, the review discusses the impacts of the professional development programmes on both teachers and students. Although many papers highlight the lack of growth in teachers (e.g. lack of knowledge about students' cultures) and the difficulty in measuring such elements after a programme, a few benefits were identified in the papers such as increased confidence in teaching culturally diverse students and the ability to connect science content with students' racial backgrounds. Very few scholars discussed the impact of the programmes on students and for those who did, few demonstrated the influence on students' test scores, for example. The authors thus suggest focusing further on the direct influence of the professional development of teachers on students.

Focusing on preparation for culturally responsive practices in the United States, Bottiani et al. (2017) identified ten studies on the impact of in-service training on teachers (and some administrators). All the studies had different foci. While some aimed at improving teacher *knowledge/beliefs* (e.g. cultural self-awareness, sometimes generalizable across student groups or focused on a specific group such the Dine Navajos, one of the largest tribes in the United States), others focused on specific *skills* such as instructional strategies and behaviour management. One reviewed study was based on several training sessions during which the teachers were made aware of how culture and context shape, for example, parental involvement in children's education, child-rearing practices and attitudes towards education. In general, the authors also show that the effectiveness of in-service interventions is not demonstrated in the reviewed papers and call for more work to be done in order to develop such tools.

In what follows, I review recent studies related to professional development from different parts of the world. In 2019 and 2021, Biasutti and colleagues evaluated the influence of training courses on intercultural education for in-service teachers in Italy and as part of an international project. In 'Social sustainability and professional development: Assessing a training course on intercultural education for in-service teachers', Biasutti et al. (2019) review a learner-centred course based on a sociocultural approach with Italian primary and middle school teachers. The course was created as part of a project sponsored by the European Union called *Educamigrant*, which aimed to support teachers in learning to act as 'facilitators in integrating the various cultural perspectives and negotiating different points of view within the classroom'; 'be fully aware of their beliefs about cultures and cultural exchanges' and 'to develop an open attitude in terms of welcoming migrant children and their families and integrating them into society' (Biasutti et al., 2019: 2–3). This is how one section of the programme is described:

> During this workshop, participants examined the different dimensions of the concept of "culture", discussing and exchanging ideas about the impact that their cultural backgrounds has on their professional activity. They were also invited to reflect on how students' culture could affect their educational experience at school. This workshop aimed to foster self-reflecting capabilities, critical thinking, self-awareness, and the adoption of a learner-centered approach in teaching. (Biasutti et al., 2019: 5)

The authors claim that, by engaging the teachers in discussions around different pedagogical approaches, teaching strategies and practices in intercultural education, the programme supported them to reflect actively on their teaching approaches and practices in relation to interculturality.

In a comparative study of Korean and US professional development in multicultural education, Choi and Lee (2020) examined the influence of programmes on teacher self-efficacy in multicultural classrooms – or their perceived ability to teach diverse students. The data used to do so was derived from the OECD Teaching and Learning International Survey (TALIS) (2018b) concerning South Korea and the United States. The survey examines how teachers and school leaders view their working conditions and learning environments at their schools. Choi and Lee (2020) found that professional development plays an important role in teacher efficacy while supporting a positive school climate. Although there are differences between South Korea and the United States, teachers are said to feel empowered to better understand students' diverse backgrounds, reduce stereotypes and promote educational justice and equity for all students. I note here (again) that perceived ability does not necessarily mean that teachers are able to teach in intercultural ways or are entirely successful at it. I also insist on the fact that, although this is a comparative study, the theoretical and conceptual knowledge about multicultural education is United States based and published in English. No theoretical and conceptual knowledge about interculturality and diversity from South Korea – a very different socio-economic-political context from the United States – is used in the paper.

The final paper presented here was published in 2019 by Hajisoteriou et al., where they discuss the impact of a six-month teacher professional development participatory course on stereotypes in Greece. This paper is included here since it is one of the only papers that focuses on a very specific approach to preparing teachers for interculturality. The course combined face-to-face and online activities. It was based on the principles of action research and reflection upon action, whereby the teachers focused on a specific inquiry in their workplace in order to improve their practice. The authors discuss how the teachers looked at their own stereotypes in relation to diversity and used their reflections for designing and implementing interventions. The course was implemented in two phases, with the second phase focusing on interaction and communication in the classroom and the role of stereotypes in them. This is how the second phase is described by the authors:

> Teachers, in a reflection process, were invited to think about their students, the relationships they develop and the factors that determine the quality of these relationships. Indicative questions used for reflection are:
> - Who are my students?
> - What do I know about them?
> - How do I negotiate their diversity?
> - Am I learning something from them?
> - How do I handle conflicts due to diversity?
> - How do I reinforce collaboration in my classroom?
> - Do I use specific strategies and techniques to combat stereotypes?
> - How do I encourage dialogue?
>
> The discussion that followed concerned the classroom as a group, its structure and function, the ascription of specific roles, and the shaping of relationship dynamics. During the discussion, teachers were invited to reflect on their experience regarding the conditions prevailing in their classrooms, how relationship dynamics are shaped and whether subgroups (cliques) are formed in their classrooms and on what basis. Teachers also discussed the ways they intervene and manage conflicts and communication problems.
>
> (Hajisoteriou et al., 2019: 180)

The authors conclude that it is difficult to evaluate the effectiveness of such a programme, since work on stereotype deconstruction is complex, requiring teachers to deal with interculturality both theoretically and practically in schools. Yet, collaborative action research, they argue, 'may thus become communities of learning and practice that offer opportunities to teachers for joint learning and application of learning on intercultural issues; developing a sense of ownership amongst participants; enhancing teachers' commitment to intercultural education and inclusion; producing and disseminating tacit know-ledge; and reflecting on teachers' intercultural practices' (Hajisoteriou et al., 2019: 185).

To conclude on professional development for intercultural teacher education, I wish to include discussions of mobility experiences. A certain number of publications have examined the impact of inter-/national (physical and/or online) mobility on pre-service teachers' sense of interculturality, as a form of professional development.

Abraham and von Brömssen (2018) report on Swedish pre-service teachers' reflections on experiences from a field study in South Africa. They show that even a short-term field study can have an impact on pre-service teachers, for example in the way they see and understand themselves and in relation to how different conditions can affect students' learning.

In 'Using telecollaboration to promote intercultural competence in teacher training classrooms in Turkey and the USA', Üzüm et al. (2020) used Byram's (1997) model of intercultural communicative competence (ICC) to examine pre-service teachers' interculturality through a telecollaborative project between Turkey and the United States. They found that the project supported the participants' emergent competence and that their awareness of heterogeneity in their own and interactants' culture, their nascent critical cultural awareness and their curiosity and willingness to learn more about the other culture were foregrounded.

Two further studies from the United States discuss the impact of time spent abroad on pre-service teachers. Starting from the premises of critical multicultural education, McBride et al. (2020) compare two versions of the same course, with one operating as a study abroad course in Trinidad and Tobago (southern Caribbean). The course is described as follows:

> Common features shared by both versions of this course include completion of the Implicit Association Test (IAT) (Greenwald et al, 1998), writing a "cultural baggage" paper, researching and facilitating class discussions on current events, conducting cross-cultural interviews, reading ethnic literature, viewing and discussing ethnic movies, attending guest presentations on diversity topics, practicing questioning skills with a panel of international students, trying ethnic cuisine, completing action projects that are outside of one's comfort zones and conducting class presentations on these projects, completing the IDI posttest, and finally, submitting a self-evaluation paper at the conclusion of the course. (McBride et al., 2020: 271)

The authors do not show systematically how different the experiences of the same course in different locations are but indicate an anecdotal positive impact on the students with experience in Trinidad and Tobago.

In a similar vein, Lash et al. (2020) focus on the development of the intercultural competence of early childhood pre-service teachers during an eight-month university-led programme, some with a Nepal field experience at, for example, a non-profit centre providing food and care for low-income families and children. Using the Intercultural Development Inventory (IDI) before and after completion of the respective programmes, they show that all pre-service students on the entire programme increased their level of intercultural competence, shifting from trivializing cultures to recognizing cultural similarities, appreciating cultural differences and interpreting phenomena taking place in a given cultural context. Some of the students who went to Nepal and benefitted from interaction with local mentor-teachers showed significant improvements in aspects of their intercultural competence. However, some of the teachers who went to Nepal but who did not interact with mentor-teachers did not seem to improve their intercultural competence. The authors conclude the article with the important question of how to sustain the development of competence when the pre-service teachers start working in schools. This question is relevant for the whole issue of professional development.

In 'Teacher education for diversity in India: Socio-educational experiences of travel to a "margin"', Raina (2021) reflects on a visit to a remote mountain region within the framework of a four-year Bachelor of Elementary Education degree programme focused on *diversity-conscious teacher education*, based in New Delhi (India). Fifteen third-year female pre-service teachers travelled to the central Himalayas in northern India, where they were asked to reflect on the issues of quality schooling, diversity and ecological living when engaging with marginalized children. Observing the children's bio-physical reality, social ecology and local knowledge systems, the teachers got to experience 'learning to be "a life in harmony with all existence" (Tagore, 1933) in which learning from nature is a central process' (Raina, 2021: 376) – far from urban settings. At the same time the pre-service teachers were urged to reflect on the influence of ways of living that exist outside the commodification of daily life or the financialized nature of education – in other words, beyond 'obvious' capitalism.

This subsection has focused on the professional development of pre- and in-service teachers, giving us a snapshot of the many and varied initiatives taken in different parts of the world for interculturality. As noted in previous subsections, specific ideologies and approaches seem to dominate the reviewed literature, and, at times, are supported by political institutions (e.g. the EU). Several questions emerged from this review:

- What kind of knowledge should be imparted to the trainees? What approach(es)? For how long should the training last?
- Who decides the content? Are participants aware of the ideological background of the training?

- Who are considered the 'targets' of the training initiatives? Students as a whole, specific groups of students (e.g. 'migrants', students of specific ethnicity, race, gender . . .)?
- What are the concrete expected outcomes? Long term and/or short term? (How) can they be 'recognized'? Do the ways of assessing learning and competence fit in the local (ideological) context?
- What are the impacts of the training on the students? Should their voices be included in discussions of what to include in professional development programmes?

Physical, face-to-face and/or online mobility was evoked in this subsection and has been examined as a potential contributor to interculturality for teacher education. For example, some papers show the benefits for teachers to observe conditions affecting learning in different contexts, as an important mirror to reflect on one's own conditions and practices. The year 2020 put a temporary end to physical mobility and few teachers had the opportunity to travel to 'learn'. Yet the opportunities afforded by online mobility (e.g. virtual exchanges with other teachers, access to classroom environments abroad via a mobile phone) could be further explored as an 'easy' way to access to other contexts and colleagues in other parts of the world.

Recent Theoretical and Paradigmatic Additions to Interculturality For Teacher Education

In this last review subsection, I present a number of emerging and recently proposed theoretical perspectives that are being used for preparing teachers for interculturality. These perspectives are often labelled as 'critical'. Certainly, all of them add new important aspects to discussions of diversity in teacher education; however, we need to bear in mind that, when faced with the idea of 'critical', we also need to be *critical towards criticality* – we will develop this argument in the next section (see Chen & Dervin, 2020; Dervin & Tan, 2022).

The idea of *the global* was discussed briefly at the beginning of this section (reference was made to Goodwin's (2020) work). As asserted earlier, trends in education around the world, under the impulsion of supranational institutions such as the OECD, for example, with the addition of global competence to PISA studies, are including discussions of the global in dealing with issues of diversity and social justice. The idea of the global is being integrated in existing curricula or being made available in stand-alone courses.

Kerkhoff and Cloud (2020) propose a Global Teaching Model where intercultural collaboration is deemed central. It is based on Kerkhoff's (2017) model for (US) K-12 educators and includes four factors:

- *It is situated* since teaching is culturally relevant in a specific class and local community.
- *It is integrated* in the sense that it is found across grade levels and disciplines – not 'isolated'. This also reminds all educational actors of the connectedness of world issues.
- *It is critical*, in reference to the systematic inclusion of issues of power, privilege and oppression in and around teaching, including for example marginalized voices in knowledge production activities.
- *It is transactional* and has to do with the concrete inclusion of the 'other', especially through international partnerships, allowing students to work and learn with people from different contexts.

Kerkhoff and Cloud (2020: 2) summarize the values of these factors as follows: 'The first two factors, situated and integrated, describe how global teaching can be connected to existing curricular structures and instructional practices. The last two factors, critical and transactional, explain how teaching about the world can be approached from a critical frame and commitment to equity.'

Besides the adjective *global*, some scholars also make use of the idea of *Global Citizenship Education*. In 2020, Estellés and Fischman proposed a review of the literature on the concept for teacher education, showing the heterogeneity of the field, with conflicting ideologies. What these initiatives try to propose is 'a deliberate attempt to go beyond narratives of nationally bound membership and to overcome the limitations of prior civic education proposals' (Estellés & Fischman, 2020: 231). The authors note that previous studies have identified many and varied trends in the way the notion is problematized, such as *neoliberal, radical and transformational approaches*; *open, moral and social-political global citizenship*; or *cosmopolitan and advocacy types of global citizenship*. They themselves identified different discourses in the way the notion was used in teacher education research. The dominant understanding seems to revolve around the idea that Global Citizenship Education is an emancipating educational solution to global problems – which the authors critically evaluate as hyperrationalized, altruistic and romanticized. They conclude by suggesting that this naïve discourse disregards factors such as the negative effects of neoliberalism and becomes as such implicitly Western. They also note that Global Citizenship Education contributes somehow to build up an elitist image of the global. Finally, the fact that very few concrete activities involving making a real difference to the world are included in teacher education initiatives leads to the use of pedagogical models that lack the political engagement that one would expect from them.

As far as the label of *multicultural education* is concerned, the adjective *critical* has also been added to it, such as by Gorski and Parekh (2020) in Canada and the United States in order to promote a perspective that takes social justice and transformative teaching into account, as well as to support the development of equity-related skills for teachers. Gorski and Parekh draw on Jenks et al.'s (2001) tripartite model of *conservative* (assimilationist perspective aiming to help the 'Other' become like 'us'), *liberal* (pluralism, promotes working on one's biases) and *critical* (placing issues of power, privilege and different form of injustices at the centre) approaches to multicultural teacher education and Gorski's (2009) five approaches based on a review of syllabi of multicultural education courses in the United States, asserting that:

> Teachers who have developed a critical lens are prepared, for example, to recognise even the subtlest ways heterosexism operates in classrooms and schools; to identify and advocate against school policies and practices that create or exacerbate gender disparities in educational opportunities and experiences; and to engage students in conversations related to poverty and economic injustice. (Gorski & Parekh, 2020: 268)

Gorski and Parekh (2020) add that teachers using a critical lens also understand how schools are impacted by bigger societal conditions such as structural racism and economic injustice. However, they note that several hindrances to implementing critical multicultural education by teachers have been observed: *instructional* (e.g. student resistance, diverse teachers themselves might feel uncomfortable), *institutional* (e.g. resistance from colleagues) and *structural* (e.g. dominance of test-prep pedagogy preventing critical views). Importantly, the two authors also warn against gaps between teachers' critical orientations versus their implementation of critical practices, whereby discursively and in terms of beliefs, they might support equity-based forms of education while in reality their teaching does not match these ideals. Without the critical elements proper, multicultural education might remain at the surface of bigger problems and provide teachers with a sense of self-confidence that is in fact inappropriate when working with diverse students.

In another paper, Gorski and Dalton (2019) speak of critical reflection in multicultural and social justice teacher education. Working from existing conceptualizations of critical reflection (mostly from the US context), the authors focus on the nature of critical reflection in assignments from diversity courses for teacher education in the United States. They identified five approaches: *amorphous 'cultural' reflection* (corresponding to the aforementioned conservative approach to multicultural education), *personal identity reflection* (encouraging students to examine their beliefs and values regarding e.g. race and class), *cultural competence reflection* (a liberal perspective which urges future teachers to adapt their teaching to the students' 'culture' without making any reference to e.g. issues of power), *equitable and just school reflection* (considered as critical, urging teachers to explore their attitudes and biases) and *social transformation reflection* (urging pre-service teachers to connect issues of justice in school with the broader socio-economic context) – with the last two appearing to be 'preferable' for the authors. Talking about teacher educators, the authors explain that 'teacher educators cannot focus solely on changing students' hearts; they must help students understand the relationships between their ideologies and the sociopolitical conditions that underlie them to help change those conditions' (Gorski & Dalton, 2019: 357). Based on other scholars' arguments, the authors list the following practices of critical reflection for teacher education, with a focus on justice-oriented change: spotting and deconstructing deficit views of underprivileged students, learning to help students develop critical media literacy, deepening their understandings of their power and privilege and, for example, starting advocating for marginalized students (amongst others).

In a similar vein, but with a focus on change in pre-service teacher practices, Liu and Ball (2019) propose a Framework of Transformative Teacher Education for Diverse Learners based on the principles of critical reflection and generativity (i.e. generation of new or novel behaviour in problem-solving). The scholars start by noting that most research on teacher education has focused on changes in beliefs, attitudes and understandings, disregarding somehow the changes these also trigger in classroom teaching practices. The authors argue that a potential consequence is 'preservice teachers talk[ing] the talk but not walk[ing] the walk' (Liu & Ball, 2019: 89). Basing their work on Liu (2015), *critical reflection with the goal of transformative action for social justice (for teachers)* is defined as:

> a process of constantly analyzing, questioning, and critiquing established assumptions of oneself, schools, and the society about teaching and learning, and the social and political implications of schooling, and implementing changes to previous actions that have been supported by those established assumptions for the purpose of supporting student learning and a better schooling and more [just] society for all children. (Liu, 2015: 144–5)

Guided by teacher educators, analysing and critiquing one's assumptions about diversity and interculturality are thus proposed as first steps. Recognizing their embedment in specific historical and cultural contexts and structures is also of importance. For Liu and Ball (2019: 92), the ultimate goal of the proposed approach consists in 'actively searching for alternatives to the ways in which diverse learners are failed by our current educational systems'. Pedagogical problem-solving to meet (oft-unknown) needs and contexts is essential here.

All in all, pre-service teachers should learn to develop as reflective, introspective, critical and generative thinkers in order to create real change in terms of practice.

On top of 'critical' perspectives, Sorkos and Hajisoteriou (2021) have proposed combining intercultural and inclusive education for teacher education in the Greek context, arguing that the dichotomy should be overcome and join forces pedagogically. They name this perspective 'sustainable intercultural and inclusive education' and place the issue of intra-generational and inter-generational inclusion, equality and social justice at its centre, as an 'area of contact' between the two. This is how they justify their move (Sorkos & Hajisoteriou, 2021: 521): 'What we argue in this paper is that active citizenship may not be substantiated only through intercultural education, but inclusive education is necessary in order to provide a socially-just character to intercultural education that also has to be sustainable'. In their paper based on discussions with teachers who were introduced to the perspective, teachers share their suggestions as to how sustainable intercultural and inclusive education could be achieved in schools. These include collaboration amongst teaching personnel (creation of interdisciplinary teams, including leadership actively), active and systematic collaboration with parents, and joint instruction with the support of specialized professionals.

The final recent perspective on teacher education and interculturality derives from a 2021 paper published by Toohey and Smythe (2022) about posthuman and decolonizing perspectives in teacher education, focusing on English as an additional language (EAL) teacher education programmes in Canada – but potentially relevant for all teachers. For the authors these perspectives could help de-centre and reconceptualize teachers' engagement with difference and diversity. Following applied linguist Pennycook (2018), posthumanism is used in the paper to refer to relational and process-oriented ontologies (explicit specification of a conceptualization), epistemologies (nature and grounds of knowledge) and ethics (morality) that move away from a human-centric view of the world, reminding us of the importance of considering other agents (e.g. objects, non-beings), rejecting in the process dualisms and binaries (nature/culture, mind/body), for example. In this perspective, differences are constructed through relations rather than 'being'. In addition to the posthuman, decolonizing perspectives aim to question first and foremost hierarchies that support coloniality. In the authors' context, decolonizing includes for example a return of appropriated land and resources but also curriculum led by members of Indigenous communities, beyond white supremacy. Epistemic decolonization, whereby knowledge systems dominated by the 'West' are put into question, is also proposed as a priority (Toohey & Smythe, 2022: 124). Considering the two perspectives together, the authors argue that posthumanism and decolonizing theories offer different and yet contingent approaches to dealing with such evils as racism and multifaceted inequalities. As an example of the two being combined for teachers, Toohey and Smythe (2022: 129) mention:

> Teacher educators Hill et al. (2020) described new teacher education assemblages emerging during COVID19, when multiple systems were pushed into chaos, 'enabling opportunities for something new to emerge' (p. 572). Changes to teacher education regulations, usually years in the making, were accomplished overnight, showing that when systems have to change, they can. The intersecting pandemics of COVID19, racism and inequality intensified in classrooms, pushing student teachers to ask 'What kind of educator do our students need us to be at this challenging time?' (p. 570).

This final subsection has allowed me to share recent contributions to knowledge about interculturality for teacher education that propose new entry points into the issue, with many claiming to be 'critical'. All of these perspectives place social justice, power and broader societal and political issues at their core, moving away from just 'culture' or 'migrants'. These perspectives require teachers to step out of their classroom somehow and to be full-time 'critical' and 'political' members of society.

The perspectives do share similarities and assumptions and note a certain number of hindrances to them being implemented in teacher education, from being used in simplified, romanticized ways to facing resistance from colleagues who do not 'buy' into them. Several questions need to be considered after acquainting ourselves with some of these perspectives:

- How compatible are they and how do such politically oriented and active perspectives fit into contexts of education which reject explicitly/implicitly politics?
- How can teachers concretely be trained to take actions against structural inequalities, for example – a 'level' of action considered as successful social justice teacher education?
- How can these rather complex perspectives be introduced through professional development programmes without simplifying, for example, their philosophical and political assumptions?
- How can teachers be 'protected' against being accused of being too political and against losing their job if 'doing' these perspectives entails taking radical actions that go against institutional legal framework?

I have met many teachers in different parts of the world who don't feel that it is their responsibility to be more 'political' in their classroom. In fact, many of them don't feel confident because they don't think they have enough knowledge about complex socio-economic issues and that they are powerless to make a difference. Some of them also refuse doing it for fear of being labelled as troublemakers by their colleagues and leadership. Who can then 'force' them to try to be more engaged with issues of 'power' and 'social justice'? Should they be 'pushed' to do it? Whose agenda(s) should they follow? A major issue here also relates to ways of speaking about these issues and the potential negative impact of copy-pasting such discussions from one economic-political context to another.

What appears to be missing in the aforementioned perspectives relates to central issues of communication and interaction – which are, in fact, at the core of the topics of power and social justice. *How to be(come) together in a classroom and in the larger context of a school? How to address and 'read' each other in educational contexts? How to ensure that everybody has the power to speak and to be listened to – and not just* heard? *How to systematically take into account, multilingual discussions in the classroom, for example, to enrich our ways of seeing the world, knowledge, and so on? And finally, how to learn* with – *rather than* from – *each other?* These all have to do with the basis of education – *communicating in education.*

Conclusion

Section 2 aimed at introducing ideas and findings from selected international research on interculturality for teacher education. We started from the simple notion of interculturality but had to enlarge and encompass other perspectives that cannot but be relevant for our purposes in this Element. Although the notion of inter-culturality is at the core of the Element, we cannot stay within just one box labelled *interculturality.* Even within this single box, there is a plethora of discordant voices. Some similarities and divergences have emerged from the different paradigms and labels used in today's research on teacher education. In general, they reflect well discussions in other fields of research in relation to diversity and in broader societal contexts (increasingly: e.g. awareness of social injustice, decolonialism).

The multiplication of terminologies and models (the 'bric-a-brac') can feel overwhelming and confusing and trying to make sense of this 'simplexity' is not an easy task. The snapshot that I presented, based mostly on literature published in the English language over a limited period of time, clearly dominated by the West, and especially the United States, reminds us that we need to beware of what we (are made to) use in teacher education. Many of the perspectives that I discussed labelled themselves as 'critical'. One of the problems that I noted again and again was the lack of criticality towards this self-proclaimed criticality. This is a major problem which challenges in a sense the 'critical' flavours of the proposed approaches. Critiques can easily become 'litanies' if we are not made to unthink and rethink them, in order to reflect on what to do concretely in action with them. We shall discuss this issue more in depth in the next section.

Teacher education and training is a privileged place to observe what is happening in a given society and globally. The proposed discourses and practices in this context reflect well certain dominant (and sometimes conflicting) views. Teacher education and training, nationally and/or globally, can also reveal current 'clashes of ideologies' and prevailing voices as far as interculturality and diversity are concerned. These usually go hand in hand – again – with broader societal positions. When one is educated/trained to be a teacher, many voices influence what we are made to think, believe in and do in our classroom: teacher educators might pass on their own beliefs and ideologies, relying on specific decision makers, supranational institutions and/or scholars. Being able to examine critically and reflexively these elements is, I propose, one important aspect of teacher education and training.

Thinking Further

About teacher education and training

– Should teachers be trained for interculturality in the same way, following one perspective only, or should they be introduced to as many different approaches to interculturality and diversity as possible, and allowed to disagree and choose how they wish to do interculturality in their classroom and beyond? What are the pros and cons of these options?
– How could we disrupt the hegemony of certain voices in discussions of interculturality for teacher education, even critical voices which have emerged in very specific contexts but do not necessarily fit in other contexts?
– Professional development can be centred around all students or very specific groups of students when it comes to interculturality. Which of these do you think fits better the purpose of preparing teachers?

About teachers and interculturality

– How would you characterize a teacher 'committed' to interculturality in their work?
– A student asked me the other day why some teachers resist and refuse to take training in diversity and interculturality issues. What are your views on this question, especially in relation to your own context?
– Both teacher educators and researchers have a lot of (symbolic) power in deciding what is good, bad, right and/or wrong for interculturality for teacher education, following at times official stances on the issues (e.g. from ministries of education). They thus impose (indirectly) their perspectives on interculturality on teachers – who might agree and/or disagree with them, feel patronized but not voice their opinions. Within the context of professional development, how could less 'imposition' take place?

- Related to the previous question, how much are teachers' (already) rich social/intercultural experiences taken into account in interculturality for teacher education? How often do you yourself use these experiences to reflect on what you do in the classroom and school environment?
- Many perspectives reviewed in Section 2 have to do with power, justice and broader societal issues. In your opinion, should teachers include discussions of and actions for change in and through their teaching? In other words, should teachers be more political?

About you

- As a practitioner, have you noticed dealing with issues of interculturality differently in the classroom, based on specific students, teaching–learning contexts and/or content? How do you explain these differences and what can one learn from reflecting on this diversity of actions and reactions?
- What we say does not always correspond to what we really want to say, and more importantly to what we say we do. What strategies could help us be more coherent in this sense? Is it even possible?
- Have you ever taken a 'test' concerning your competences to deal with interculturality and diversity? What was it like? Did you identify certain ideologies and/or beliefs in the test that you disagreed with? What did you think of the results? And, more importantly, what did you learn from taking the test?
- If you consider yourself to be 'critical', how do you understand this word in relation to interculturality for teacher education? Do you think that you are also critical of your own criticality and allow for oppositions in your discussions with others about interculturality? Can you think of instances?
- How dedicated are you to the issues of, for example, social justice and anti-discrimination in your work? How do you understand what they entail concretely? Do you have concrete examples of how you have proceeded with them?

3 Critical and Reflexive Interculturality in Practice

Objectives

- To reflect on what we can do with the 'bric-a-brac' of terminologies and ideologies from the international literature published in English discussed in the previous section;
- To learn to take into account contextual and linguistic discussions of interculturality;

- To learn to make informed choices about the way we problematize, discuss and put interculturality into practice in our teaching and research;
- To build up systematic curiosity for diverse takes on interculturality to enrich our own thinking.

Reflect Before Reading the Section

- In the previous section we discussed many different terms used to deal with interculturality in teacher education (e.g. *critical multicultural education, culturally relevant pedagogy, global teacher education, social justice education*). At this stage, which term do you seem to have a preference for? Can you explain why? Also, are you now aware of the (complex) ideological backgrounds of the term and of its archaeology?
- Why do you know what you think you know about interculturality? Where is that knowledge from?
- There are probably aspects of interculturality-work and -talk that you may not feel comfortable with at this stage. For example, you may find it difficult to understand what your role as a teacher (educator) or even as a researcher has to do with 'social justice', beyond the context of the classroom. What other aspects covered in the previous section do you feel you would need to reflect on or be further guided in?
- Many of us work in multilingual contexts but might use one or two (dominant) languages in our work. Try to evaluate the consequences of this limitation on your engagement with interculturality. For example, as a teacher educator, using dominant Western knowledge about interculturality derived mostly from the literature published in and translated from English, and trying to use it in local contexts, what is it that we might be missing when ignoring issues of multilingualism and translation in the way we present that knowledge?

From *Efficient* to *Critical and Reflexive*

In spring 2022, a symposium on the education of young people in China and Germany took place in Beijing. The aim of the two-day symposium was to make suggestions as to how to prepare these young people for interculturality. This was expressed as: 'to cultivate the ability of young people from both countries to conduct intercultural exchanges and have mutual understandings' (China Daily, 2022). One of the keynote speakers is quoted as having said:

> "Therefore, intercultural communication and collaboration grow to be very important currently," he said. "At this point, it's significant for us to discuss how to empower teenagers by honing their understanding and communication

skills as well as tapping into their potential to bring up efficient international cooperation in the future." (China Daily, 2022)

Nothing was said in the media report about how all these key terms were understood: 'mutual understandings'; 'understanding and communication skills'; 'efficient international cooperation'. Of special interest here are the claims of nurturing 'efficiency'.

One of my favourite novels was written by Gustave Flaubert and is entitled *Bouvard and Pécuchet: A Tragi-Comic Novel of Bourgeois Life* (1904). In the novel, two friends aim to write a book about every subject in the world (agriculture, biology, chemistry, gymnastics, politics, etc.) by educating themselves in every possible field. However, their overly ambitious and unrealizable project ends in disaster as they become engulfed by the complexity of knowledge available. I like this novel because it reminds us of the importance of being modest, realistic and focused. As was seen in Section 2, tens of different answers are available in research on how to prepare teachers to both guide students in their path to interculturality and to trigger interculturality in school environments. A veritable 'jungle of terms' was noted and I claimed that this could be somewhat overwhelming for teachers, teacher educators and even scholars who wish to look into interculturality. However, unlike *Bouvard and Pécuchet* we should not be overly distracted by this 'simplexity' but be encouraged to move forward. Diversity is at the heart of interculturality and so should it be regarding the way we conceptualize and problematize it.

Many of the approaches mentioned in Section 2 overlap, while others differ in the ways scholars spoke of what to expect from interculturality and what to do about it in teacher education. From my observation, these 'answers' – and the ideological perspectives that they carry – do also get mixed, modified and adapted around the world. All of these perspectives are embedded in broader political issues and influenced by specific economic-political contexts, which might be very localized at times and more global at others. In most countries, teachers should refrain from (visible, obvious) political engagement and while the perspectives discussed in the previous section often place ideas and concepts within specific political arenas, I believe that many of us are unaware of this indirect influence, which is sometimes on the verge of indoctrination. This puts us in situations whereby we are asked to do politics without being fully aware of it. We might rehearse discourses of *social justice, tolerance, democracy* and *equity/equality*, for example, without really knowing what these mean concretely, what they entail and if the background ideological positions of the voices we follow are in fact compatible with what we are asked to do as educators in our own contexts. These discussions remind me of a play by Eugène Ionesco called

The Lesson (1951), a comedic parable of the dangers of indoctrination. In the absurd one-act play, a professor uses the meaning he gives to words to dominate over an eager female student. The following excerpt shows well how this tyrannical behaviour functions in the play (Ionesco, 1958: 1360):

PROFESSOR: [...] Tell me now, by simple deduction, how do you say "Italy" in French?

PUPIL: I've got a toothache.

PROFESSOR: But it's so easy: for the word "Italy," in French we have the word "France," which is an exact translation of it. My country is France. And "France" in Oriental: "Orient!" My country is the Orient. And "Orient" in Portuguese: "Portugal!" The Oriental expression: My country is the Orient is translated then in the same fashion into Portuguese: My country is Portugal! And so on...

I am not saying here that we scholars are trying to indoctrinate others when we speak of interculturality. I am suggesting however that, if we are not careful and do not 'evaluate' how, why and what scholars assert about interculturality, we might find ourselves in the same situation as the pupil in Ionesco's play.

One argument that the review from the previous section identified was that scholars often claimed that interculturality for teacher education seems to be an eternal challenge, which, I think, is a good thing. There is no simple answer of to how to 'do' and conceptualize interculturality. There is in fact a need to continue thinking about the notion and to move forward together, complexifying it and multiplying the voices addressing the issues we face. The snapshot of studies from Section 2 represents a good and useful basis for us to see where we position ourselves as scholars and practitioners within the global field and to enrich our thoughts and practices.

A few reminders about what we are doing with interculturality in this Element are needed before we proceed to my proposals.

First of all, let us remember that we are dealing with interculturality as *an object of research and education* (i.e. how we conceptualize it and make use of it) rather than interculturality as a personal endeavour for meeting other people. This is a very important distinction since my interest is not in telling you, for example, how you should behave with different 'actors' in school contexts or how you should judge what is 'good' or 'bad' intercultural communication.

Secondly, the work of the teacher is a highly complex one since it includes all kinds of tasks and responsibilities. In what follows we shall discuss aspects of interculturality that are relevant for the following situations (note that the 'boundaries' between these elements are not as obvious as one might think):

- *Inside the classroom*: for example, working and socializing with students; students–teachers mediating togetherness; engaging ourselves and students with knowledge interculturally by, for example, addressing knowledge asymmetry by questioning overly 'Western' knowledge and offer alternatives.
- *In school*: for example, cooperating and socializing with students from other classes, leadership, colleagues and other staff; engaging with knowledge produced within the school in relation to the outside world.
- *Outside school*: engaging and mediating with parents, others and knowledge (social media, the news etc.).

Our classrooms and research contexts are always diverse – every classroom, every teaching–learning act, every research initiative, involve interculturality one way or another – and the way we see interculturality might differ immensely from the ways others see it. What is more, interculturality does not stop at the door of one's classroom or when we exit the school; it goes well beyond and affects us all. We thus need to take into account diverse viewpoints on interculturality in our work. In this section I am not going to tell you how to think about interculturality but will let us think further about it, while stimulating a habit of being critical and reflexive about the notion. I will step off from the position of the omniscient writer here – the one who knows it all and gives orders to readers. Obviously, like all other scholars I have my own (ideological) preferences as to what interculturality could mean and how we can 'do' it as educators and scholars. But I must refrain from imposing these ideas, derived from my own position as a 'European' scholar who has navigated between ideologies from French *interculturalité* (based on the centrality of laïcité – 'secularism' – and similarities over differences), Finnish multiculturalism (a soft and liberal form of American multiculturalism, with a rather vague form of 'Nordic' social justice) and the broad ideologies of 'critical interculturality' from some parts of the West (non-essentialism, non-culturalism, i.e. refraining from 'solidifying' people into cultural boxes). I might reveal some of my own take at the end of the section but it won't be meant to be considered as 'the' approach to adopt. Aspects of it can be tried out but, as we shall see in the section, it is always important to ask questions and to consider them from different angles.

This section is more creative than the previous one and derives directly from the remarks we made about the international literature and from my own practice as a teacher educator and researcher in a context (Finland) where teacher preparation is research based and aims at stimulating reflexivity and criticality in future teachers – rather than providing them with 'ready-made' or 'miraculous' solutions. I have thought of ways to reflect together with the reader on how to move forward, how to take into account what we learnt from Section 2 – from all the simplex fund of knowledge – and to try to go further without fixing an end point. In order to help us think beyond the box, I make use of ideas and arguments from the arts and literature, using them to form conceptual metaphors. As asserted in the introduction, I also make many references to Chinese thought, as a way of decentring our thinking about aspects such as diversity and language. Having interacted with Chinese colleagues and students for many years now, I wish to share some of my learning beyond my own 'corner' of the world. I do encourage readers to think of examples, illustrations and ideas from other non-Western contexts as they read through this section.

My main goal here is to guide you through some of the questions that we might need to engage with when we consider interculturality in teacher education. With all this knowledge available on the market, with researchers having their own preferred labels, theories and references, one might be wondering who to turn to, 'follow' or even who is 'right' or who is 'wrong'. These questions are not of interest here. As such there is no right or wrong, as long as we are able to evaluate the knowledge produced by those we read. One thing is for sure though: we must avoid falling into the trap of perspectives that offer what I would refer to as *one-sided criticality* – that is, not being critical of itself, its own pros and cons, its ideologies and its own criticality.

Four Conceptual Metaphors to Make Sense of and Use Interculturality in Teacher Education

In what follows we review four conceptual metaphors to help us problematize what we could do to examine interculturality reflexively and critically and to take (fluid) actions accordingly (see Figure 1): *the three steel towers, the advent calendar of interculturality, knights' move on a chessboard* and *the language kaleidoscope*. Conceptual metaphors consist of two cognitive structures: a source domain (e.g. an object or a work of art in what follows) and the target domain (aspects of interculturality) (see e.g. Lakoff & Johnson, 1980). The following conceptual metaphors will help us understand how to 'do' interculturality critically and reflexively.

Metaphor 1: The Three Steel Towers

Imagine that you are standing in a gigantic hall, where three nine-metre-high steel towers have been installed (see the middle of Figure 1). At the bottom of each tower there is a spiral staircase leading to a viewing platform with large circular mirrors on top of each tower. You can climb up to the platforms with other people (colleagues, friends, strangers, your students, their parents…). Each of the three towers has a name: *I Do, I Undo* and *I Redo*. In this work of art

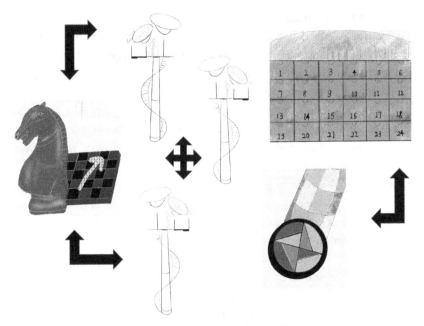

Figure 1 Four conceptual metaphors.

presented in London in 2000, artist Louise Bourgeois (1911–2010) wanted the visitors to experience intimate and significant encounters while reflecting on themselves and these encounters. The large mirrors were meant to reflect the encounters and discoveries between the participants and the towers to those watching at a distance from an elevated bridge in the hall. This was meant to give visitors the experience of self-conscious anxiety, under the spotlight and in company of others and the public gaze. Going up each tower, spending some time on the platform and looking into the mirrors, you start reflecting critically on what you 'do' (Tower 1), how to 'undo' (Tower 2) and how to 'redo' (Tower 3). Alone or together with other people you start looking into yourself and the way you (have been made to) think about and conceptualize interculturality, and how others have dealt with this process. In Tower 1 you ask yourself, looking into the mirror: *what is interculturality about for me and for the people around me? Who is interculturality about? What words do I associate with interculturality? What values do I attach to doing interculturality in my job as a teacher/researcher? How does this influence me in the way I teach, act and socialize within my educational context? Do I remember situations where I 'did' interculturality well and others where I failed?* And then you start asking yourself: *what is it that I am not fully satisfied with in the way I think about interculturality? For example, what concepts have I been using which I feel are not suited or useful for moving forward? What is it that I would like to change about my take on interculturality? How can I work actively with others to do so?* Tower 2: going up the tower together with others and looking into the mirror concretizes the undoing of interculturality by discussing and reflecting actively on others' take on the notion: *what has influenced me concretely in the way I see interculturality? How do people around me see and do interculturality? How different and similar from me? What words do my colleagues, students and their parents, for example, use in our shared language(s) and other languages to talk about it? What can I learn with them to undo my habits and ways? Amongst the different perspectives on interculturality available in the literature, which ones can I explore further and why?* When you enter Tower 3, the process of redoing starts. You can try out new ideas, new concepts, new ways, as renegotiated with others in Tower 2. Before entering the tower, you can also ask those who were observing at a distance from the bridge for feedback and suggestions: *how did they view my looking into the mirror alone and/or with others? What can I learn with them too?* You might also want to relate your reflections from the towers to your own life experiences, to your encounters with people outside the school context. Although we have been made to believe sometimes that there is a 'border' between what happens in school, for example, and outside, we need to revise this assumption. Elements of our biographies, of who we are, of our life experiences – which Roland Barthes calls 'biographemes' (1971: 175) or snapshots of autobiography – should be integrated in our reflexive work.

Since interculturality is a lifelong endeavour, which requires adapting constantly and testing and adopting other ways of 'doing' it, entering the third tower does not mean that the process is over. Redoing does not signal that we are ready and that we can grasp and 'do' interculturality forever. No perspective on interculturality will ever be strong or perfect enough to withhold its complexities. On the contrary, when we exit the third tower, we need to go back to the first one and start the process again: *do, undo* and *redo*. Every time we try out new things or when we face situations that indicate surprise or failure, we need to go back to the first tower.

When I have discussed this 'never-ending' process of going from one tower to another, many of my pre-service teachers have deemed it not to be a very positive metaphor. Some have compared it to the myth of Sisyphus, whereby one pushes a boulder up a hill, which goes back down systematically and one is doomed to push it back up forever. However, this complex process of reflexivity, pushing oneself to reflect on how one does, undoes and redoes, is essential to interculturality in teacher education. As we have seen in the previous section, wishing to engage with the notion (and the tens of other such notions used in education), we can never be sure that what we (are made to) think is adequate. The use of different terms and ideologies requires us to be careful, to listen to what others and ourselves say and 'do' about interculturality and to open our mind to other ways of thinking about it. Reflexivity, whereby I go back to what I think, say and do, to observe what seems to work and to make changes, is a 'natural' way of being: we reflect all the time on ourselves, others and the world, sometimes openly, other times without realizing. As such, we often 'talk to ourselves' when we act or when we have to make decisions. For Confucians, for example, reflexivity is central to our self-cultivation and moral integrity. For instance, the Chinese philosopher Master Zeng (505–436 BCE), a disciple of Confucius, uttered in the *Analects*:

> Master Zeng said, "I daily examine myself on three counts – whether, in serving others, I have been wholeheartedly devoted (zhong 忠); whether, in interacting with friends, I have been not trustworthy (xin 信); whether, having been given instruction, I have not practiced accordingly." (In Ni, 2017: 86)

This gave an idiom in Chinese: 三省吾身, *reflect on oneself several times a day, with the intention of improving oneself*. The idea of improving oneself is an important one, yet, what it means for doing interculturality as an educator should not be considered as a static 'thing'. What the three steel towers metaphor might indicate here is that improving oneself through reflection is endeavouring to the following elements: 1. Observing and going back to what one thinks and does; 2. Observing and paying particular attention to what others say and do as far as interculturality is concerned; 3. Redoing as one enriches one's take on interculturality through engagement with others (enriching here refers to considering other ways of thinking and doing it *ad infinitum*, adapting to individuals and contexts).

Metaphor 2: The Advent Calendar of Interculturality

The second metaphor I would like to use has nothing to do with religion here. I am merely using it as a way of making an important point for our work as educators. The advent calendar is a 'countdown' calendar to a holiday called *Christmas*. Usually made of cardboard and containing pieces of chocolate or other surprises, it is composed of small doors with numbers (one to twenty-four) that one opens each day before Christmas day. Although I am not a Christian, when I was a child my parents bought such a calendar every year, and every single day we would get excited at the idea of opening one of the doors to discover the surprise of the day. I like this metaphor to describe the sort of curiosity and excitement that we should experience as far as interculturality as an object of research and education is. Obviously, the advent calendar needs to be modified for exploring interculturality: there is no ending date, the number of doors is unlimited and one does not need to follow the order of door numbers.

Discovering other (disrupting/inspiring) ideas, concepts and notions, ideologies and ways of expressing things about interculturality should be part of our job. Realizing that 'my' interculturality is not necessarily 'your' interculturality, such as in the way we define it or discuss what it entails, cannot but enrich our ways of engaging with the notion. The more perspectives, ideas and concepts I discover about interculturality, from all parts of the world and in different languages, the more I am able to think critically and reflexively about what I think and do, thus supporting myself in navigating between the aforementioned steel towers. In a book by another Chinese Confucian philosopher, Xunzi (c. 300–230 BCE) of the same name, a chapter is entitled 'Dispelling Obsessions' (解蔽), which starts with the following assertion: 'The affliction most people have is that they are obsessed with one corner and cannot see the big picture' (Xunzi, 2013: 521). The advent calendar forces us to look for and be curious about the 'big picture' of interculturality to interrogate our 'corner'. On top of the perspectives that were reviewed in Section 2, limited to the broad context of intercultural teacher education, one could include doors to lesser-known perspectives from different parts of the world: for example, *Dowa* in relation to overcoming prejudice and economic injustice from Japan; *Ubuntu* based on the idea of human connectedness from South Africa; or the *Minzu* perspective on diversity in unity from China (see e.g. Dervin & Yuan, 2021; Dervin & Jacobsson, 2022). Due to space constraints I cannot introduce these somewhat '*terrae incognitae*' here but urge the reader to get acquainted with their complex specificities and to 'taste' the linguistic components in the ways they are problematized and constructed (see e.g. Dervin, 2022b about 'Chinese stories of interculturality').

Besides research perspectives which can give us a strong and stimulating basis in exploring complex ways of engaging with interculturality, we should also be encouraged to open doors to, for example, the arts, literature and travel. All these have to do with interculturality and listening to a piece of music and reading about the composer's life and discussions of the piece, for instance, can open up our mind about interculturality. Using our ears, eyes and other senses to rethink interculturality can inspire us in new ways. Many artists, composers and writers have influenced me in my doing, undoing and redoing of interculturality (in alphabetical order and selectively): (music) *Pierre Boulez, Sophia Gubaidulina, Kaija Saariaho, Igor Stravinsky, Tan Dun*; (art) *Marina Abramovic, Marcel Duchamp, Xu Bing*; (literature) *Elias Canetti, Fyodor Dostoevsky, Sadeq Hedayat, Eugene Ionesco, Lao She*. Artists, musicians and writers from all over the world can often add interesting dimensions that can bridge the gaps that one might find between what scholars write about and the complexities of our life experiences.

Educators and researchers are very busy and some readers might be wondering how to cultivate such curiosity with so little time. Obviously, the advent calendar requires time and one does not need to invest so much energy all at once since the process is lifelong. A notebook that I bought in China reads in English: 'Don't have to choose. Let it be!'. What I find fascinating with the advent calendar metaphor is that randomness and chance are the best companions. I have myself discovered what I consider to be life-changing individuals, ideas and perspectives by chance. *Just be curious and let it be!* But remember to take notes, to write diaries in the language(s) you know and to use what you find behind the doors for exploring the three steel towers.

Metaphor 3: Knights' Move on a Chessboard

As educators and scholars interested in interculturality, through the towers and the advent calendar we find the motivation and strength in ourselves to ask questions – without always having answers – and to have doubts about what we think we know about the notion. These processes can be performed by ourselves (e.g. diaries, blog entries, notes) and with others (e.g. discussion groups, peer assessment). An important part of the process is to ask questions and question knowledge about interculturality. Again, as seen in Section 2, a wide range of knowledge has been produced around the world, but knowledge from the West seems to dominate the complex field of intercultural communication education.

Here we use the metaphor of the knight in chess, inspired by a quote from Canetti (2021: 211): 'In growing, knowledge changes its shape. True knowledge knows no uniformity. All leaps in knowledge occur sideways: the way knights move on a chessboard.' In chess, knights can move in an L-shaped manner over the board. It is the only piece that moves this way and for beginners it is difficult to move the piece – especially as it goes counter to the way we have been made to think about 'moving forward'. This metaphor reminds us of the importance to look for knowledge (moves) elsewhere, to consider positions and directions that we might not have envisaged before. It also suggests moving away from following the same pattern and the orthodoxy of interculturality (from Greek: *orthodoxia*, 'right opinion'). The knight metaphor also urges us to be careful of not blindly following certain moves, certain voices, certain 'big names', certain concepts and notions. For example, *ideological mimetism* whereby I might rehearse words and phrases to define interculturality and its 'application' needs to be deconstructed. We all use certain words related to interculturality which we may not necessarily be able to demarcate. These might include, for example, the concepts and ideas of *tolerance, respect, intercultural competence/citizenship*, *democracy* and *social justice*, which are all polysemic within and between languages, and embedded in specific economic-political contexts which give them flavours that one may not recognize in other places. Although we'll come back to the aspect of language in the next subsection, I want you to reflect at this stage on each of these words: *what do they mean to you concretely? What do they tell you and others to (not) do in relation to interculturality? What/who has influenced you in the way you understand them? Are you aware of other ways of defining and using them? How do you use them in your work as an educator?*

Now let's think about how to move sideways like knights.

Moving in an L-shaped manner as far as interculturality is concerned consists first of all in practising our skills in independent thinking. Being aware of what the dominant discourses on interculturality are globally, I 'dig into' the advent calendar and explore alternatives and voices, which are often cut off from view, such as the ones mentioned earlier (e.g. Minzu, the arts). The more doors I open, the stronger I become, the readier I am to undo and redo my take on interculturality. The more training I receive in unsettling my thoughts, the more I can move beyond my own intellectual comfort. In the process, I can jump over pieces and discard them (words, ideologies, objectives. . .). In Chinese, the idiom 东施效颦 indicates that it is unnecessary to imitate something which is not suitable for us since it could be counterproductive to adopt it. Such 'conflicts' can be sources of newness in the way we negotiate the notion of interculturality, talk about it and act upon it with others. This kind of move can also increase minor voices' power to speak and their right and power to be listened to.

The concept of *discourse* has been used in research on interculturality to examine what people say about how they conceptualize and 'do' it – but more specifically how they position themselves in relation to the notion. For Heny and Tator (2002: 25), 'Discourse is the way in which language is used socially to convey broad historical meanings. It is language identified by the social conditions of its use, by who is using it and under what conditions. Language can never be "neutral" because it bridges our personal and social worlds.' When one examines the etymology of the word discourse, one notices that it comes from Latin *discursus* for 'a running about' and *discurrere* 'to run about, run to and fro, hasten'. 'Discoursing' is thus running here and there, moving in all directions with words. As Henry and Tator put it (2002: 25), as a consequence, 'language can never be "neutral"'. Talking about interculturality in any language and in specific contexts, we might reveal a lot about our own ideologies and beliefs – see our biases. Because discourse is always embedded in other people's discourses, we also often face being contradictory in what we say (e.g. 'I have no stereotypes about Finns but in general I think that they are a bit shy').

In Chinese, the word contradiction is 矛盾. The character 矛 stands for *a spear* and 盾 for *a shield*. So, in Chinese, the word *contradiction* opposes a shield and a spear – a deadly weapon versus protective gear. Going back to the knight metaphor, we need to bear this image in mind when we listen to the discourses of others and our own discourses about interculturality. Criticality is here central. When we use the word *critical* in research and education, what we mean by it is not always clear. What is more, often claims of criticality seem to disenfranchise us from being critical of our own criticality, which ends up putting us in the same position as the ouroboros, the snake that eats its own tail. *Criticality must be critical of itself!* When we move sideways like the knight, we must remember to look back and to reflect on our moves and the decisions we made to move in a certain direction. Again, using certain 'critical' words, concepts and ideas 'robot-like', without undoing them, will not necessarily lead to us moving forward in the way we think about interculturality, and, in fact, will have little influence on how we'll 'do' interculturality with others.

Criticality of criticality means being sensitive to discourses, to the way we put words into motion to talk about interculturality. In what follows, I suggest focusing on the following issues as a start.

When we engage with interculturality as an object of research and education, we often use 'pet' terms and ideas – which we may discard or keep as we move along in our lifelong engagement with the notion. As a consequence, there are many terms that we ignore, are unaware of or even condemn in our own language(s) and other languages. As a complex glocal notion, this is always bound to happen. We need to reflect constantly on why we (are made to) use and prefer certain terms over others, as I have discussed earlier. In this process, we also need to beware of what I call *interculturalcentrism* – believing that 'our' way of thinking and speaking about interculturality is the only 'right' and 'valid' one. I can think of two examples that I witnessed recently: a European scholar asserting that papers which contain the word 'race' should not be published because the word does not mean anything and is dangerous in education; an American scholar laughing when I suggested that we should consider the construct of *harmony* when we speak about interculturality, which he labelled as 'very Chinese', thus 'naïve' and 'fake'. When I asked him how he defined *harmony* and what he knew about the way it was used in China, he mumbled a very unconvincing answer about harmony having to do with uniformity and conformity – a common stereotype about the Chinese! What he did not know was that the Chinese word (和谐) should be translated as *diversity in harmony*, indicating that harmony is about balancing otherness with otherness and refuting sameness. The knight move here is for us to be curious of and accept that things might be labelled differently, and refrain from belittling them, rejecting them hastily or naming them 'less developed' or 'less interesting'. 'The demon of generalizations' (Nabokov, 2019: 55) is never far away. Some countries are often presented and constructed as not fitting in to the cookie cutter of being good at diversity/interculturality. However, we must listen to them and observe reflexively before judging.

Observing discourses (ours and others) also requires questioning what appears to be the accepted, the obvious, the taken for granted, and asking questions about them.

Practising the metaphor of the knight moves should not happen alone. We need to engage with others in educational contexts and beyond. We need to move across to the other (etymology of the word *dialogue*), hoping that others will also move across to us. Depending on our status and 'power', we also need to be able to stand up to others and to ask questions about why we should understand a term or a learning objective in a certain way, and to dig deeper into the meaning of things. Discussions with teacher educators and decision makers are important here. The right to disagree and suggest changes should be respected. For example, in Finland, many teachers have been trained to use certain frameworks related to interculturality proposed by supranational institutions like the Council of Europe since the early 2020s. Having attended some workshops, I noticed that very few teachers questioned for example the 'replacement' of the idea of *interculturality* with *democratic culture* and that they swiftly shifted to the use of the latter. Ideologically, there is a difference between these terms, and their use will have an influence on how we speak as educators, passing this knowledge on to the next generations. The aforementioned Ourobouros syndrome (the snake eating its own tail) is an issue that we need to seriously take into account and try to avoid as much as we can if we want to make interculturality meaningful and transformative. For us researchers this also means listening carefully to education actors (students and parents included) and to avoid speaking over them in the way they discuss interculturality. When reporting our research, we must also be critical of our own criticality and avoid 'judging' teachers, for example, with our own ideological take on interculturality. Again, we are all involved in interculturality, and any teacher having spent thousands of hours in a classroom already has a strong sense of the complexities of interculturality from which we can all learn.

Metaphor 4: The Language Kaleidoscope

As the reader will have noticed, I often make references to language in discussions of interculturality for teacher education. Some of us will have access to a certain number of languages, sometimes from the same language family, sometimes from different language families. We might be able to read, speak, listen to and/or interact in some of these languages. Some of us might have access to one language only. Whichever situation we are in, it is only through and with language that we can discuss and make sense of such a complex object as interculturality. And it is only through direct and/or indirect interaction with other people that we do. Using language is never an 'easy business' as it requires constructing thoughts and ideas, negotiating meanings (again and again), transforming and (at times) manipulating what we say and hear. The writer Svetlana Alexievich (2016: 30) summarizes this complex process as follows:

> I'm searching for a language. People speak many different languages: there's the one they use with children, another one for love. There's the language we use to talk to ourselves, for our internal monologues. On the street, at work, while travelling – everywhere you go. You'll hear something different, and it's not just the words, there's something else, too. There's even a difference between the way people speak in the morning and how they speak at night.

Reading Alexievich's take on language, one is easily reminded of the fact that speaking in one or several languages, interlocutors, motivations for speaking, locations, moods ... impact on how we speak and what we speak about. One could use the image of the *master* and *slave* to describe our daily relations to language, with others.

One could say that the same applies to the way we engage with the notion of interculturality. As a polysemic, economic-political construct, if we deal with it in our own language(s) or in a global academic language like English, the end results (i.e. how able we are to come to a joint understanding, how we 'do' interculturality) might differ depending on who we are talking to and the place in which we are located (amongst others). When we speak about interculturality, we always need to remember that what we mean might be interpreted completely differently by our interlocutors and that they contribute to meaning making as much as we do. For instance, we might use a word in English as a lingua franca that connotes differently to them (e.g. *tolerance, diversity, inclusion*). As such, the very word *interculturality* might be difficult to render in other languages. In Chinese and Finnish for instance, the notion might be substituted by *multicultural* or *transcultural*, since the root *inter-* is not necessarily available in these languages or is 'awkward'. It is thus important to allow time to negotiate these aspects of language when working with colleagues, teachers and/or other scholars.

The metaphor I use here is that of the language kaleidoscope. A kaleidoscope is a cylinder-type instrument. It contains pieces of coloured glass, which are reflected in an endless variety of patterns, by means of mirrors placed inside the cylinder. The word, from Greek, means *a variety of beautiful shapes/colours*. In Chinese, the word is translated as 万花筒, which refers to *ten thousand* (万) *flowers* (花) in *a cylinder* (筒).

Reading through the literature on interculturality, as we did in Section 2, we can notice that some elements of criticality, for example, proposed by some researchers do not stand the test of the language kaleidoscope, especially if limited to the English language treated as a monolith. The words that we use to discuss interculturality might be understood and connoted differently when we step outside our own economic-political sphere – although they might also be perceived and used differently by other people within the same sphere. Words used for interculturality are inherently polysemic, although they might appear 'simple', 'straightforward' and 'to be taken for granted'. Some words dominate global research, as we have seen earlier. Baggini (2018: 107), for instance, reminds us that 'When an American politician speaks in praise of freedom, it is because the culture demands that the value of freedom is upheld, just as in China it is harmony which must be defended.' What these terms mean for the ones who utter them and the (complex) range of local and global receivers is a real issue to consider seriously. Obviously, I am not suggesting a totally differentialist approach here, whereby what we say about interculturality in one language and multilingually will not be understood and/or understandable – there are similarities across contexts. However, I do believe, based on my interactions with people from many different parts of the world, that we should never take words, phrases and discourses for granted, especially if they encompass specific ideological positions – which they often do for such a political concept as interculturality.

Looking into the language kaleidoscope of interculturality, whereby we try to identify multiple patterns for a single word (a concept, a notion) or an idea (an assertion about interculturality), we realize first and foremost that some are used as mere clichés ('prêt-à-parler', *ready-to-speak*) and never really explicated or positioned. In other words, some terms are treated like automatons, either because of their popularity in research, education and politics, or because the utterer 'likes' the word.

In the Finnish educational context for instance, the words equality (*tasa-arvo*) and social justice (*oikeudenmukaisuus*) are now omnipresent. Finnish scholars working on the issues publish about these issues in English but never question the meanings and connotations of these words globally, using mostly (implicit) definitions from the United States or the UK. One could ask first if the adopted definitions make 'full' sense within the Finnish discourse ecology. And then, what does the idea of *tasa-arvo/equality*, as used in these publications, bring to mind to a scholar in Japan, Nigeria or Chile, for example? How do they interpret research results from the Finnish context? What are the potential consequences of misunderstanding the 'colours' of the words in English as a lingua franca?

In a recent research project application that I reviewed in Finland, the candidate was using the phrase 'culturally diverse pupils' throughout. As I moved forward in the application, I was expecting some kind of definition of 'culturally diverse'. However, the explanation never came. I was left wondering who the phrase referred to. Obviously, knowing the discourse ecology of Finland on this issue I assumed that this was a way of referring to (certain groups of) 'migrants' with a disadvantaged socio-economic background or 'children of migrants' (who might be Finnish citizens). If someone from Ghana, the Philippines or Kazakhstan, for example, who did not know anything about the Finnish context, had read the application, what would they have made of the phrase?

The Chinese artist Xu Bing has dedicated a lot of his work to the issue of language and to the illusions of communication. Two of his pieces can be used here to further understand the points that I am making here. In 'Book from the Sky' (ca. 1987–91), one sees rows and rows of 'Chinese characters' on large pieces of fabric hanging from the ceiling. To someone who cannot read Chinese, this all looks 'authentic' and many visitors will marvel at the beauty of 'Chinese writing'. However, if one can read Chinese, one notices, the closer one gets to the characters, that they are in fact not real Chinese characters but invented forms of Chinese writing. I have seen Chinese speakers being very confused by the experience as they imagined first that they were seeing their own language. In another piece entitled 'Square Word Calligraphy' (1994–6), Xu Bing mixed the Latin alphabet with the 'format' of Chinese characters to create an entire new writing system. Using three to four alphabet letters, he made up a Chinese character. So, for instance the characters for Shanghai are composed of one character with S, H, A, N, G and another one with H, A, I, arranged in such a way that they both look like Chinese characters. Again, the viewer gets perplexed by this new writing, but, unlike the first piece, is able to 'read' the characters when they learn to decipher them. Often, when one reads and engages with interculturality one can experience the same illusions: one sees a word, a concept or a notion, assumes its meaning and connotation, but may get it completely wrong because the writer might have had other meanings and connotations in their mind. The reader's lack of awareness of a given economic-political context, and of the ways interculturality is dealt with in politics, education and research in other contexts might make the situation even more confusing.

Another important consequence of the lack of interest and care for the language kaleidoscope is the exclusion and distortion of other knowledge. By assuming that everyone understands and uses words in the same way to 'deal with' interculturality, one closes the door to potential disagreement and thus enrichment of knowledge. If the polysemic values of equality, equity and social justice matter, we should start by caring about language, and opening up doors to joint understanding. We need to liberate ourselves from ways of speaking about interculturality which give us the illusion of a-contextuality (applies to all regardless of where they are located), a-politicality (concepts and notions do relate to glocally embedded ideological positions) and universality (e.g. English as a 'neutral' global language).

Beyond the most widespread words used in English (and then in other languages, in more or less satisfactory translated versions), glocal contexts might have their preferences for certain terms that might be difficult to render in other languages and/or be considered of no importance by outsiders. These include, for example, *harmony* (China, Singapore), *reconciliation* (Australia), *laïcité* (France), *transfronterizx* (United States) and *community* (different parts of the world for different purposes). When we use such terms in English and/or other languages, we need to make sure that we present enough of the contextual backgrounds and the connotations of the words to be understandable.

This leads me to the last point about the language kaleidoscope: *translation*. Today, although translation is omnipresent, there is very little discussion around the topic in teacher education, as if translation was a given. Translation is a process that we use every day without even realizing. Sometimes we even 'translate' within 'our' own language(s) to try to make sense of the world. When one starts paying attention to translation, one notices that the words for interculturality are indeed complex. As Kraus (1990: 67) puts it: 'The closer the look one takes at a word, the greater the distance from which it looks back.' Including translation as a vital component of the kaleidoscope does not mean that one needs to be a professional translator or speak many languages. Online technologies offer excellent tools that can support us in this process, to try to dig deeper into the words that we and others use, to try to come to a potential understanding. For Lahiri (2022: 7) 'translation goes under the skin and shocks the system'. This has been my take on the topic ever since I started working with Chinese colleagues. At the beginning of our cooperation, we tended to be 'polite' and to agree with each other, without ever questioning what we were saying, and especially the words and phrases that we used to discuss interculturality in English. One day, I realized that this was a wrong approach because we did not seem to be able to 'communicate' around the notion, and were just acquiescing. I could feel that something was wrong, that the words that we used together such as *ethnicity*, *civilization*, *development* and even *propaganda* were not the same. We thus decided to examine all the words that we had been using, decomposing each and every one of them in Chinese, English, French and Finnish. We soon realized that we had been 'deaf' and 'blind' to the diversity of (hidden) connotations that we had been giving to the words in English. This 'went under my skin'. Let me give a simple example. As asserted before, I have done a lot of work on the notion of Minzu (民族) in Chinese education. The very word can be translated in at least three different ways in English: *ethnic groups*, *nations* or *nationalities*. I have seen these words being used interchangeably in publications in English and in official translations in China. With my Chinese colleagues, we have come to the conclusion that, in fact, none of these words describe well enough the realities of the Chinese context and that outsiders will get confused by the English words. What we have also realized is that the three words would bring to mind a certain number of ideological perspectives and realities that are 'alien' to the Chinese context. As a consequence, we use the Chinese word *Minzu* in our work and systematically explain what it means within the context of the Chinese mainland.

This is what the kaleidoscope can help us do: to look at words and the way things are formulated through different lenses. It also supports us in avoiding explicit or implicit ideological impositions on the way we think about various aspects of interculturality. What the kaleidoscope tells us is that we need to translate again and again, and especially to *translate translation*, that is, to beware of the use of certain words and phrases that might not be fitting. The kaleidoscope calls for us to be sensitive to words – not to ban or censor their use, this would make no sense – but to understand why we perceive words to mean or connote in certain ways, to be clear about why we (wish to) use them and to undo and redo the words with others so we can move forward in our path to interculturality as teachers.

To finish this subsection on language, I suggest that you reflect on the following questions. The kaleidoscope goes hand in hand with the three previous metaphors (*the three steel towers, the advent calendar, knights' move on a chessboard*) and is meant to accompany the critical and reflexive work of engaging with interculturality in teacher education:

- How would you define interculturality at this stage? Pay special attention to every single word that you use to define it: what do they all mean? Why do you think you chose these words to define interculturality this way? Are some of these words 'pet' words to you? Why? What other words could you have chosen (in different languages)?
- Next time you engage with a school leader, a colleague and/or a parent, try to listen carefully to the way they phrase how they see interculturality. What

words do they use? Do they seem to use these words in meaningful ways? What do these words tell you about their take on the notion? What are the potential ideologies hiding behind what they say?

- Look around the educational context where you work and try to identify slogans, mottos and discussions that have to do with any aspect of interculturality. What do they reveal about the institution ethos? How do these fit in your own take on interculturality?
- Think about the words and phrases related to interculturality that appear to be omnipresent in your own context (media, school, friends, business). Which of these words or phrases might be difficult to translate into other languages? Why? Can you try to think about ways of explaining them to someone who does not speak the language in which they appear.
- Finally, when you hear the following words and phrases, what 'colours' come to your mind? Are these words that you often use as a teacher? *Social justice, diversity, ethnicity, race, harmony, freedom* and *democracy*.

On the Importance of Thinking Otherwise about Interculturality in Teacher Education

Every night before going to bed I practise three simple and yet difficult exercises: 1. Using a calligraphy brush, I write three sentences from something I read during the day, using my weakest hand (left). 2. I try to picture what my day was about 'backwards', starting from the moment I am about to go to bed to the moment I woke up. 3. I pick up my phone, open the Kindle app, click on any book, open a page and turn the phone upside down and start reading for a couple of minutes. These exercises seem to push me outside my comfort zone, enabling me to experience my realities differently and to 'revise' the way I have visualized and conceptualized them. This is not a miraculous set of practices but it reminds me every day that I need to undo and redo the 'done', the taken for granted, the obvious, and look back.

In this section we have reviewed four metaphors offered as ways of guiding us in undoing and redoing interculturality (*ad infinitum*) in teacher education. The steel towers, the advent calendar, the knight's moves as well as the language kaleidoscope, like the simple exercises described above, are not miraculous recipes – there can't be any for such a complex, ever-changing and ideologically driven notion as interculturality. How we engage with the notion as teachers, teacher educators and scholars depends (in-)directly on our (complex) life experiences; the quality of life; our status in a given institution; our own political, religious, societal, scientific and educational positions and views (amongst others); other people's views (with which we may disagree or not);

how we see our place in the world and, especially, how we have been made to see it (e.g. through official curricula). Many other elements might also influence our views such as our health, our mood and our level of stress. It is easy to see how and why we construct and reframe interculturality *throughout our lives –* rather than once and for all. All the elements listed here change and make us change. At times, depending on where we are located, who we are interacting with and how much (diverse) knowledge we acquire, we might consider inter-culturality to be about the encounters between the 'majority' and 'minority', about 'locals' and 'migrants', about indigeneity, race and/or a combination of identity markers, and we might deem it 'doable' in changing ways, considering, for example, tolerance, equality or unity as major goals. The metaphors can help us reflect on these processes by considering the notion *otherwise* but they will never give us 'right answers'. For me, interculturality urges us to fight against our fear of change and to jump in and out of ideas, identities and ideologies, leaving space for (dis-)comfort, joy and anxiety, but also contradictions and some degree of (in)coherence.

If I could summarize what we have attempted to do in this section, I would say that the more I question the way(s) I have been made to think about interculturality the more I am ready to open up my understanding and dealing with the notion, thus accepting the complexities of self and other when engaging with it.

Thinking Further

– I used four metaphors in this section to guide us through criticality and reflexivity concerning interculturality. Can you think of alternative meta-phors to describe, for example, the need to 'do', 'undo' and 'redo' and the importance of reflecting on language in the construction of interculturality?
– Foucault (1998) has looked into how we construct and reflect self (and other) by means of what he named 'technologies of the self', that is, objects and practices that help us look into oneself and discuss what we find. These could include today: *writing diaries, expressing oneself on social media (Facebook, Twitter, Weibo), conversations with close friends but also with total strangers, writing reflexive essays at school, reading and physical exercise as a way of stimulating self-reflexivity.* In a way, the three steel towers metaphor is another form of technology of the self. Can you think of other such technologies of the self that you could make use of to reflect on interculturality as an educator?
– What comes to your mind in relation to the discussions in this section when you read the following four quotes from three different individuals (an artist, a philosopher and a writer)?

o 'Men of convictions are prisoners.' (Nietzsche, 2018: 58)
o 'I force myself to contradict myself in order to avoid conforming to my own taste.' (Duchamp in d'Harnoncourt & McShine, 1973: 16)
o 'The calamity of knowledge when it is passed on unchanged.' (Canetti, 2021: 26)
o 'Try not to judge. Describe. There is nothing more disgusting than condemnation. It's always this way or that and it's always wrong. Who knows enough to judge another? Who is selfless enough?' (Canetti, 1989: 102)

4 Piecing Together the Jigsaw of Interculturality

Objectives

- To summarize discussions and takeaways from the Element;
- To reinforce relating previous research on interculturality and one's own take on the notion;
- To provide further questions that can guide us in being critical and reflexive about interculturality in teacher education and training.

At a recent conference on global competence and teacher education in English, I was surprised to hear many speakers and participants repeat sentences such as 'students should be tolerant', 'students should learn about other cultures', 'students should be critical thinkers'. These were neither problematized nor explained. I asked the audience: *we are all giving 'orders' to students now, but what about us teachers? Do we know what all these mean and, more importantly, how to 'do' them?* My questions were met with complete silence.

In this Element we have discussed the (necessarily) 'elastic' concept of interculturality. In Section 2 we reviewed some selected literature on interculturality for teacher education (and its companions such as *multicultural* and *global*). Many publications were identified in the English language, with a certain number of research and ideological strands dominating the way scholars spoke of interculturality. We noted that most of these perspectives had to do with 'glocal' economic-political contexts and that the words used to describe how 'things' should be and done were not always clearly demarcated, leading at times to prosaic or overly polysemic use. We discussed the potential danger of being unaware of both the meanings/connotations of some concepts, notions and values in different contexts and of contextual characteristics when we try to 'copy-paste' such endeavours. Amongst the topics covered in the reviewed papers, of interest for our purpose were: discussions of the need to include epistemic diversity in what we teach; the central role played by teacher educators in introducing pre-service teachers to issues of interculturality; the need to take into account educators' previous experiences in allowing them to reflect on the notion (*international, glocal mobility* included) and the importance of professional development.

Based on my practice of reflexivity and criticality as a teacher educator and researcher in Finland, Section 3 was meant to serve as a basis for 'self-professional development'. In fact, one of the problems noted by the scholars from Section 2 was both the inconsistency and the inequality or lack of access to teacher professional development around issues of diversity and interculturality in education. Section 3 was not meant to help readers 'deal with' interculturality as a personal endeavour but to think, unthink and rethink together the way we conceptualize the notions. For example, going back to the conference mentioned at the beginning of this conclusion, while making statements about what students 'should do', educators and researchers should actively interrogate the words they use, discuss them with those concerned and present their listeners with 'open', 'complex' and 'in-the-making' definitions. This is what we explored in this Element: how can we continuously conceptualize and make use of interculturality as *an object of research and education*? As educators (teacher educators, pre-service and in-service teachers but also scholars), it is our duty to pay attention to this important aspect of our work, rather than passing on 'orders' (ideologies, Roucek, 1944) on to people that we do not necessarily understand ourselves and are unable to 'perform'. This reflects better, I believe, the complexities of the work of the teacher. Constantly we are pulled apart between different situations, responsibilities, tasks and interactions. A one-size-fits-all way of thinking about and engaging with interculturality could never support us 'successfully', especially as interculturality is always something that we do and conceptualize (implicitly or explicitly) with others inside and outside the school context. It is this central aspect of our work that requires us to shift from 'knowing it all' about interculturality to modestly undoing and redoing it with others all the time.

I used four metaphors in Section 3 to help us engage with interculturality critically and reflexively. Table 4 summarizes what to take away from the discussions around the metaphors.

Let me finish with two concepts that I have found very inspiring to summarize what we are attempting to do with interculturality here.

The first concept was coined by the German writer Bertold Brecht (1898–1956): the *alienation* or *estrangement effect* (in German: *Verfremdungseffekt*). As a writer for the theatre, Brecht wanted his audience to experience something special while watching his plays (Brecht, 1964: 94). The alienation effect was meant to present the 'familiar' in unfamiliar ways so that the audience did not

Table 4 How to 'do' critical and reflexive interculturality.

What to do?	How?
Ask questions to yourself and others	Doubt what you/they think you/they know or have been made to think about interculturality
	Step aside and back (alone and/or together with others)
	Unsettle your thoughts
	Don't necessarily look for answers
Be critical of (your own) criticality	Look for signs of *interculturalcentrism*
	De-universalize, realize and accept that 'your' interculturality is not necessarily 'their' interculturality
	Question indoctrination and orthodoxies ('slogan-esque' statements, motto-like arguments)
	Analyse clashes of ideologies
	Deconstruct 'pet' theories and concepts
	Belittle your belittling when you believe that a word or an idea concerning interculturality is not worth considering
	Accept dissonance and antagonism
Be curious	Explore other ways of engaging with interculturality
	Listen to silences in the ways interculturality is discussed
	Enrich yourself with knowledge about interculturality, through, for example, the arts, fiction and/or philosophy
	Focus on differilitudes (differences + similitudes) between your ideas and others'
	Use this curiosity to trigger curiosity in others
Care about language	Translate again and again (translations)
	Give real meanings to words
	Unearth ideologies hidden behind words
Listen	Let others enjoy their power to speak
	Undo and redo *together with* others
	Accept the unpredictable while listening to others

empathize with the story but, instead, thought profoundly about the play in social-critical terms. This distancing effect was produced by using 'strange' and 'unusual' theatrical techniques such as actors stepping out of character to lecture, summarize or sing songs and stage designs representing a-locality.

By so doing, the audience was asked to participate actively in the play by, for example, asking questions and relating what was happening on stage to real-life events (Brecht, 1964: 95). The alienation effect is very close to the reflective and critical perspective on interculturality that is proposed here: as educators, we need to step aside, to make the familiar unfamiliar and to become more active in the production (rather than mere re-production) of knowledge and perspectives on interculturality. Although *alienation* or *estrangement* might sound negative to some readers because of the way they perceive the words *alien* (from Latin *alius* for 'another, other, different') or *strange/r*, I believe that they reflect very well the 'mirror effect' or the 'treating oneself as a stranger' that I have tried to promote in this Element.

The second concept, related to alienation, is from the Chinese language: 诸子学. This translates in English as 'Study a Hundred Schools of Thought'. 诸子学 refers to the work of scholars during the period from the late Spring and Autumn Period (around 476 BCE), which experienced disintegration of the old social order, through to the early Han Dynasty (around 206 BCE). Because of the collapse of the social order and values, scholars engaged in deep and free thinking to try to propose solutions for the big problems their societies were facing. This period led to the emergence of a large number of 'schools of thought': Agriculturalism, Confucianism, Daoism, Mohism, Syncretism (amongst others). Although a comparison to these times would be anachronic and unjustified, I believe that the principle of studying a hundred schools of thought is inspiring for unthinking and re-thinking interculturality in precarious times like ours. I hope that this Element, which represents a snapshot of my ideas, co-constructed indirectly and directly with the colleagues, friends and students that I have had the pleasure of cooperating with over the years, will contribute modestly to augment our interests in 'a hundred schools of thought of interculturality'.

Thinking Further

To conclude the Element, I would like us to reflect one last time on what I consider to be the most important questions to ask ourselves when engaging with interculturality. These are not meant to be static or unique questions and I do encourage you to spend time devising your own important questions, identified through practising the four metaphors. Ideally, the questions we ask about the notion should be considered in interaction with other people (face to face or, for example, through social media). As mentioned earlier, any actor located within an educational institution is a precious source of interrogation on interculturality: students themselves, their parents, support staff, colleagues, cleaning staff, psychologists, pastoral care specialists, counsellors, leaders, members of the school board, sponsors, and so on. Always consider their perspectives, opinions and own (often extremely rich) experiences to 'shake' your own views. Consider the differilitudes (both differences and similitudes) between what you think and do and what they think and do. The verb *to consider* shares the same root as the adjective *considerate* (i.e. to be thoughtful of the rights and feelings of others). Both words come from Latin *considerare* 'to look at closely, observe', with *con* meaning 'with, together' and *sidus* referring to 'stars' and 'constellations' ('to observe the stars'). Through this constant engagement with others, using the four metaphors as guidelines, I can reflect on how we can and might *become together* and reflect on the change we can experience together in the way we do, undo and redo interculturality. Change is part of who we are as human beings (e.g. Bergson, 1946) so observing change is not easy because it happens all the time. However, using three Chinese words/phrases related to change, we might find clues as to how it occurs between and within us as far as interculturality as an object of research and education is concerned: 化 can translate as *turn, melt, transform, expend* and *change into*. It indicates gradual and subtle change; 变 means *change, become, transform* and *vary*, pointing at manifest and obvious change; 潜移默化 can be translated as *silent transformations, unknowingly changing*. This idiom from a Confucian scholar reminds us that we go through quiet and unconscious transformations when we experience new things (see Dervin, 2022a). I argue that observing change in relation to interculturality from these three different perspectives, while considering the answers we provide to the following questions, can be rewarding. The following three sets of questions represent a summary of what to take away from the Element and can be used for regular self- or peer-reflection each year:

1. What does my educational context clearly ask me to 'do' in relation to interculturality? What are the keywords used in policies and other official documents such as textbooks? Do I understand them? How compatible are my own views and understanding, and those of others around me, with these ideologies? How can I potentially reconcile them?
2. How do I perceive interculturality? How would I like it to be done and spoken of? How about my interlocutors and people around me? What are the differences and similarities between our ways of thinking and speaking about it? What is it that we agree or disagree on? What is it that we seem to silence around the notion? How could we renegotiate a common way of seeing the notion, bearing in mind our power differentials?
3. Am I aware of any potential 'pet' researchers, concepts, ideas or slogans that guide me in the way I problematize interculturality? How much do I know about their ideological, political and worldview backgrounds? How can

I 'undo' some of my own conceptual reflexes and clandestine preconceived ideas which might blind me in the way I 'do' interculturality in my classroom, for example? Where can I look for alternatives and new inspiration to challenge myself (and others)? Is there space in my institution to have dialogues around the polysemy of interculturality as an object of research and education?

References

Abdallah-Pretceille, M. (1999). *L'éducation interculturelle*. Paris: PUF.

Abraham, Y. G. & von Brömssen, K. (2018). Internationalisation in teacher education: Student teachers' reflections on experiences from a field study in South Africa. *Education Inquiry 9*(4), 347–62, https://doi.org/10.1080/20004508.2018.1428035.

Alexievich, S. (2016). *Second-Hand Time*. New Delhi: Juggernauts Books.

Aman, R. (2017). *Decolonising Intercultural Education: Colonial Differences, the Geopolitics of Knowledge, and Inter-epistemic Dialogue*. London: Routledge.

Aragona-Young, E. & Sawyer, B. E. (2018). Elementary teachers' beliefs about multicultural education practices. *Teachers and Teaching 24*(5), 465–86, https://doi.org/10.1080/13540602.2018.1435527.

Baggini, J. (2018). *How the World Thinks: A Global History of Philosophy*. London: Granta Books.

Barthes, R. (1971). *Sade, Fourier, Loyola*. Paris: Seuil.

Beljanski, M. & Dedić Bukvić, E. (2020). Comparative overview of the presence of intercultural education of teacher trainees in Serbia and Bosnia and Herzegovina. *Journal of Ethnic and Cultural Studies 7*(3), 1–16, https://doi.org/10.29333/ejecs/412.

Bennett, J. M. (2004). Turning frogs into interculturalists: A student-centered developmental approach to teaching intercultural competence. In Goodman, R. A., Phillips, M. E. & Boyacigiller, N. (Eds.). *Crossing Cultures: Insights from Master Teachers* (pp. 312–42). London: Routledge.

Bergson, H. (1946). *The Creative Mind*. New York: Philosophical Library.

Beutel, D. A. & Tangen, D. (2018). The impact of intercultural experiences on preservice teachers' preparedness to engage with diverse learners. *Australian Journal of Teacher Education 43*(3). http://dx.doi.org/10.14221/ajte.2018v43n3.11.

Biasutti, N., Concina, E. & Frate, S. (2019). Social sustainability and professional development: Assessing a training course on intercultural education for in-service teachers. *Sustainability 11*(5), 12–38, https://doi.org/10.3390/su11051238.

Bottiani, J. H., Larson, K. E., Debnam, K. J., Bischoff, C. M. & Bradshaw, C. P. (2017). Promoting educators' use of culturally responsive practices: A systematic review of inservice interventions. *Journal of Teacher Education 69*(4), 367–85, https://doi.org/10.1177/0022487117722553.

Brecht, B. (1964). *Brecht on Theatre*. New York: Hill and Wang.

Byram, M. (1997). *Teaching and Assessing Intercultural Communicative Competence*. Clevedon: Multilingual Matters.

Canetti, E. (1989). *The Secret Heart of the Clock*. New York: Farrar, Straus and Giroux.

Canetti, E. (2021). *The Agony of Flies*. New York: Farrar, Straus and Giroux.

Castro, A. J. (2010). Themes in the research on preservice teachers' views of cultural diversity: Implications for researching millennial preservice teachers. *Education Researcher 39*(3), 198–210, https://doi.org/10.3102/0013189X10363819.

Chen, N. & Dervin, F. (2020). Afterword: Beyond the naïve mantra of criticality in education (research)? In Simpson, A. & Dervin, F. (Eds.). *The Meaning of Criticality in Education Research: Reflecting on Critical Pedagogy* (pp. 215–21). London: Palgrave Macmillan. https://doi.org/10.1007/978-3-030-56009-6_9.

Chen, N. & Dervin, F. (2023, in press). 'The more we know, the more we feel what we know is limited' – Finnish student teachers engaging with Chinese students' ideas about culture, language and interculturality. In Tavares, V. & Skrefsrud, T-A. (Eds.). *Challenges and Opportunities Facing Diversity in Nordic Education*. Lexington Books.

Cherng, H.-Y. S. & Davis, L. A. (2017). Multicultural matters: An investigation of key assumptions of multicultural education reform in teacher education. *Journal of Teacher Education 70*(3), 219–36, https://doi.org/10.1177/0022487117742884.

China Daily (2022). Symposium centered on educating German and Chinese teenagers concludes. 14 April 2022. https://enapp.chinadaily.com.cn/a/202204/14/AP62578c23a3104446d8d15c92.html.

Choi, S. & Lee, S. W. (2020). Enhancing teacher self-efficacy in multicultural classrooms and school climate: The role of professional development in multicultural education in the United States and South Korea. *AERA Open 6*(4), 1–17, https://doi.org/10.1177/2332858420973574.

Civitillo, S., Juang, L. P., Badra, M. & Schachner, M. K. (2019). The interplay between culturally responsive teaching, cultural diversity beliefs, and self-reflection: A multiple case study. *Teaching and Teacher Education 77*, 341–51, https://doi.org/10.1016/j.tate.2018.11.002.

Cobb, W. & Bower, V. (2021). *Language Learning and Intercultural Understanding in the Primary School: A Practical and Integrated Approach*. London: Routledge.

Cochran-Smith, M. & Villegas, A. M. (2015). Studying teacher preparation: The questions that drive research. *European Educational Research Journal 14*(5), 379–94, https://doi.org/10.1177/1474904115590211.

Council of Europe (2018). *Reference Framework of Competences for Democratic Culture*. www.coe.int/en/web/campaign-free-to-speak-safe-to-learn/reference-framework-of-competences-for-democratic-culture

Cushner, K., McClelland, A. & Safford, P. (2006). *Human Diversity in Education: An Integrative Approach*. New York: McGraw Hill.

d'Hanoncourt, A. & McShine, K. (1973). *Marcel Duchamp*. Philadelphia, PA: Philadelphia Museum of Art.

Deardorff, D. K. (2006). The identification and assessment of intercultural competence as a student outcome of internationalization at institutions of higher education in the United States. *Journal of Studies in International Education 10*(3), 241–66, https://doi.org/10.1177/1028315306287002.

Dervin, F. (2016). *Interculturality in Education*. London: Palgrave.

Dervin, F. (2022a). *Interculturality in Fragments: A Reflexive Approach*. London: Springer.

Dervin, F. (2022b). Introduction. In Yuan, M., Dervin, F., Sude & Chen, N. *Change and Exchange in Global Education: Learning with Chinese Stories of Interculturality* (pp. 1–17). London: Palgrave Macmillan.

Dervin, F. & Jacobsson, A. (2022). *Intercultural Communication Education: Broken Realities and Rebellious Dreams*. Singapore: Springer.

Dervin, F. & R'boul, H. (2022). *Through the Looking-glass of Interculturality: Auto-critiques*. (Encounters between East and West). Singapore: Springer International Publishing AG.

Dervin, F. & Tan, H. (2022). *Supercriticality and Intercultural Dialogue*. Singapore: Springer.

Dervin, F. & Tournebise, C. (2013). Turbulence in intercultural communication education (ICE): Does it affect higher education? *Intercultural Education 24*(6), 532–43.

Dervin, F. & Yuan, M. (2021). *Revitalizing Interculturality*. London: Routledge.

Dervin, F., Moloney, R. & Simpson, A. (Eds.) (2020). *Intercultural Competence in the Work of Teachers: Confronting Ideologies and Practices*. London: Routledge.

Dervin, F., Sude, Yuan, M. & Chen, N. (2022). *Interculturality Between East and West: Unthink, Dialogue, and Rethink*. London: Springer.

Erickson Cornish, J. A., Schreier, B. A., Nadkarni, L. I., Henderson Metzger, L. & Rodolfa, E. R. (Eds.) (2010). *Handbook of Multicultural Counseling Competencies*. Hoboken, NJ: John Wiley.

Estellés, M. & Fischman, G. E. (2020). Who needs global citizenship education? A review of the literature on teacher education. *Journal of Teacher Education 72*(2), 223–36, https://doi.org/10.1177/0022487120920254.

Ferguson-Patrick, K. & Jolliffe, W. (2018) *Cooperative Learning for Intercultural Classrooms: Case Studies for Inclusive Pedagogy*. London: Routledge.

Fitchett, P. G., Starker, T. V. & Salyers, B. (2012). Examining culturally responsive teaching self-efficacy in a preservice social studies education course. *Urban Education 47*(3), 585–611, https://doi.org/10.1177/004208591 2436568.

Flaubert, G. (1904). *Bouvard et Pécuchet*. Paris: G. Charpentier et E. Fasquelle.

Foucault, M. (1998). *Technologies of the Self*. Boston, MA: University of Massachusetts Press.

Fylkesnes, S. (2017). Whiteness in teacher education research discourses: A review of the use and meaning making of the term cultural diversity. *Teaching and Teacher Education 71*, 24–33, https://doi.org/10.1016/j.tate.2017.12.005.

Gay, G. (2010). *Culturally Responsive Teaching: Theory, Research and Practice*. New York: Teachers' College Press.

Goodwin, A. L. (2020). Globalization, global mindsets and teacher education. *Action in Teacher Education 42*(1), 6–18, https://doi.org/10.1080/01626620.2019.1700848.

Gorski, P. C. (2009). What we're teaching teachers: An analysis of multicultural teacher education coursework syllabi. *Teaching and Teacher Education 25*(2), 308–18, https://doi.org/10.1016/j.tate.2008.07.008.

Gorski, P. C. & Dalton, K. (2019). Striving for critical reflection in multicultural and social justice teacher education: Introducing a typology of reflection approaches. *Journal of Teacher Education 71*(3), 357–68, https://doi.org/10.1177/0022487119883545.

Gorski, P. C. & Parekh, G. (2020). Supporting critical multicultural teacher educators: Transformative teaching, social justice education, and perceptions of institutional support. *Intercultural Education 31*(3), 265–85, https://doi.org/10.1080/14675986.2020.1728497.

Guyton, E. M. & Wesche, M. V. (2005). The Multicultural Efficacy Scale: Development, item selection, and reliability. *Multicultural Perspectives 7*(4), 21–9, https://doi.org/10.1207/s15327892mcp0704_4.

Hajisoteriou, C., Maniatis, P. & Angelides, P. (2019). Teacher professional development for improving the intercultural school: An example of a participatory course on stereotypes. *Education Inquiry 10*(2), 166–88, https://doi.org/10.1080/20004508.2018.1514908.

Hammer, M. R. (2009). The intercultural development inventory. In Moodian, M. A. (Ed.). *Contemporary Leadership and Intercultural Competence* (pp. 203–18). New York: Sage.

Henry, F. & Tator, C. (2002). *Discourses of Domination: Racial Bias in the Canadian English-Language Press*. Toronto: University of Toronto Press.

Holliday, A. (2010). *Intercultural Communication and Ideology*. London: Sage.

Holm, G. & Londen, M. (2010). The discourse on multicultural education in Finland: Education for whom? *Intercultural Education 21*(2), 107–20, https://doi.org/10.1080/14675981003696222.

Holm, G. & Zilliacus, H. (2009). Multicultural education and intercultural education: Is there a difference? In Talib, M., Loima, J., Paavola, H. & Patrikainen, S. (Eds.). *Dialogs on Diversity and Global Education* (pp. 11–28). New York: Peter Lang.

Hummelstedt-Djedou, I., Zilliacus, H. & Holm, G. (2018). Diverging discourses on multicultural education in Finnish teacher education programme policies: Implications for teaching. *Multicultural Education Review 10*(3), 184–202, https://doi.org/10.1080/2005615X.2018.1511341.

Ionesco, E. (1958). *The Bald Soprano and Other Plays*. New York: Grove Press.

Jenks, C., Lee, J. O. & Kanpol, B. (2001). Approaches to multicultural education in preservice teacher education: Philosophical frameworks and models or teaching. *The Urban Review 33*, 87–105, https://doi.org/10.1023/A:1010389023211.

Jensen, B., Whiting Feinauer, E. & Chapman, S. (2016). Measuring the multicultural dispositions of preservice teachers. *Journal of Psycho-educational Assessment 36*(2), 120–35, https://doi.org/10.1177/0734282916662426.

Kerkhoff, S. N. (2017). Designing global futures: A mixed methods study to develop and validate the Teaching for Global Readiness Scale. *Teaching and Teacher Education 65*, 91–106, https://doi.org/10.1016/j.tate.2017.03.011.

Kerkhoff, S. N. & Cloud, M. E. (2020). Equipping teachers with globally competent practices: A mixed methods study on integrating global competence and teacher education. *International Journal of Educational Research 103*, 1–17, https://doi.org/10.1016/j.ijer.2020.101629.

Kraus, K. (1990). *Half-Truths & One-and a-Half Truths*. Chicago: The University of Chicago Press.

Lahiri, J. (2022). *Translating Myself and Others*. Princeton, NJ: Princeton University Press.

Lakoff, G. & Johnson, M. (1980). *Metaphors We Live by*. Chicago: Chicago University Press.

Lash, M., Madrid Akpovo, S. & Cushner, K. (2022). Developing the intercultural competence of early childhood preservice teachers: Preparing teachers for culturally diverse classrooms. *Journal of Early Childhood Teacher Education 43*(1), 105–26, https://doi.org/10.1080/10901027.2020.1832631.

Liu, K. (2015). Critical reflection as a framework for transformative learning in teacher education. *Educational Review 67*(2), 135–57, https://doi.org/10.1080/00131911.2013.839546.

Liu, K. & Ball, A. F. (2019). Critical reflection and generativity: Toward a framework of transformative teacher education for diverse learners. *Review of Research in Education 43*(1), 68–105, https://doi.org/10.3102/0091732X18822806.

McBride, A. E., Bellamy, D. E. & Knoester, M. (2020). The theory and practice of developing intercultural competence with pre-service teachers on-campus and abroad. *Theory Into Practice 59*(3), 269–78, https://doi.org/10.1080/00405841.2020.1739957.

Mie.ie. (2022). Postgraduate Programme in Education. www.mie.ie/en/study_with_us/postgraduate_programmes/master_in_education_studies_intercultural_learning_and_leadership_/.

Nabokov, V. (2019). *Think, Write, Speak*. London: Penguin.

Ni, P. (2017). *Understanding the Analects of Confucius*. New York: State University of New York Press.

Nieto, S. & Bode, P. (2018). *Affirming Diversity: The Sociopolitical Context of Multicultural Education*. New York: Pearson.

Nietzsche, F. (2018). *The Antichrist*. Mineola, NY: Dover Publication Inc.

OECD (2010). *Educating Teachers for Diversity: Meeting the Challenge*. Paris: OECD.

OECD (2018a). PISA 2018 Global Competence. www.oecd.org/pisa/innovation/global-competence/.

OECD (2018b). TALIS 2018 data. www.oecd.org/education/talis/talis-2018-data.htm.

Oulu.fi (2022). Intercultural Teacher Education. www.oulu.fi/en/apply/bachelors-intercultural-teacher-education.

Pais, A. & Costa, M. (2020). An ideology critique of global citizenship education. *Critical Studies in Education 61*(1), 1–16, https://doi.org/10.1080/1750 8487.2017.1318772.

Parkhouse, H., Lu, C. Y. & Massaro, V. R. (2019). Multicultural education professional development: A review of the literature. *Review of Educational Research 89*(3), 416–58, https://doi.org/10.3102/0034654319840359.

Peng, J. & Dervin, F. (2022). Dealing with moments of crisis interculturally in educational virtual exchanges: A Sino-Finnish case study. *Education Sciences 12*(9), 602. https://doi.org/10.3390/educsci12090602.

Pennycook, A. (2018). *Posthumanist Applied Linguistics*. Oxford and New York: Routledge.

Porto, M., Houghton, S. A. & Byram, M. (2017). Intercultural citizenship in the (foreign) language classroom. *Language Teaching Research 22*(5), 484–98, https://doi.org/10.1177/1362168817718580.

Puttick, S., Nye, Z., Wynn, J., Muir, L. & Hill, Y. (2021). Student teachers' beliefs about diversity: Analysing the impact of a 'diversity week' during initial teacher education. *Teacher Development 25*(1), 85–100, https://doi .org/10.1080/13664530.2020.1854336.

R'boul, H. (2021). North/South imbalances in intercultural communication education. *Language and Intercultural Communication 21*(2), 144–57. https://doi.org/10.1080/14708477.2020.1866593.

Raina, J. (2021). Teacher education for diversity in India: Socio-educational experiences of travel to a 'margin'. *Journal for Critical Education Policy Studies 19*(2), 370–90.

Roiha, A. & Sommier, M. (2021). Exploring teachers' perceptions and practices of intercultural education in an international school. *Intercultural Education 32*(4), 446–63, https://doi.org/10.1080/14675986.2021.1893986.

Roucek, J. S. (1944). A history of the concept of ideology. *Journal of the History of Ideas 5*(4), 479–88.

Rowan, L., Bourke, T., L'Estrange, L., L'Estrange, T., Brownlee, J. L., Ryan, M., Walker, S. & Churchward, P. (2021). How does initial teacher education research frame the challenge of preparing future teachers for student diversity in schools? A systematic review of literature. *Review of Educational Research 91*(1), 112–58, https://doi.org/10.3102/0034654320 979171.

Solehuddin, M. & Budiman, N. (2019). Multicultural competence of prospective preschool teachers in predominantly Muslim country. *Cakrawala Pendidikan 38*(3), 438–51.

Sorkos, G. & Hajisoteriou, C. (2021). Sustainable intercultural and inclusive education: Teachers' efforts on promoting a combining paradigm. *Pedagogy, Culture & Society 29*(4), 517–36, https://doi.org/10.1080/14681366.2020 .1765193.

Spitzberg, B. H. & Changnon, G. (2009). Conceptualizing intercultural competence. In Deardorff, D. K. (Ed.). *The SAGE Handbook of Intercultural Competence* (pp. 2–52). Thousand Oaks, CA: Sage.

Sue, D. W. & Sue, D. (2013). *Counseling the Culturally Diverse: Theory & Practice*. New York: John Wiley.

Tabatadze, S., Gorgadze, N., Gabunia, K. & Tinikashvili, D. (2020). Intercultural content and perspectives in school textbooks in Georgia. *Intercultural Education 31*(4), 462–81, https://doi.org/10.1080/14675986.2020.1747290.

Tambyah, M. (2019). Intercultural understanding through a 'similar but different' international teaching practicum. *Teaching Education 30*(1), 105–22, https://doi.org/10.1080/10476210.2018.1453795.

Tan, H., Zhao, K. & Dervin, F. (2022). Experiences of and preparedness for Intercultural Teacherhood in Higher Education: Non-specialist English teachers' positioning, agency and sense of legitimacy in China. *Language and Intercultural Communication 22*(1), 68–84, https://doi.org/10.1080/ 14708477.2021.1988631.

Thapa, S. (2020). Assessing intercultural competence in teacher education: A missing link. In Westerlund, H., Karlsen, S. & Partti, H. (Eds.). *Visions for Intercultural Music Teacher Education* (pp. 164–76). London: Springer.

Toohey, K. & Smythe, S. (2022). A different difference in teacher education: Posthuman and decolonizing perspectives. *Language and Education 36*(2), 122–36, https://doi.org/10.1080/09500782.2021.1980002.

University of Houston. (2022). Multicultural Studies in Education. www.uhcl .edu/academics/degrees/multicultural-studies-in-education-ms.

University of Nevada. (2022). Equity and Diversity in Education. www.unr.edu/ education/academic-programs/graduate-degrees/equity-diversity-and-language-education.

Üzüm, B., Akayoglu, S. & Yazan, B. (2020). Using telecollaboration to promote intercultural competence in teacher training classrooms in Turkey and the USA. *ReCALL 32*(2), 162–77, https://doi.org/10.1017/S0958344019000235.

Uzunboylu, H. & Altay, O. (2021). State of affairs in multicultural education research: A content analysis. *Compare: A Journal of Comparative and International Education 51*(2), 278–97, https://doi.org/10.1080/ 03057925.2019.1622408.

Wikan, U. (2002). *Generous Betrayal. Politics of Culture in the New Europe.* Chicago: University of Chicago Press.

Wyant, J., Tsuda, E. & Yeats, J. T. (2020). Delphi investigation of strategies to develop cultural competence in physical education teacher education. *Physical Education and Sport Pedagogy 25*(5), 525–38, https://doi.org/ 10.1080/17408989.2020.1746252.

Xunzi (2013). *Xunxi.* New York: Columbia University Press.

Yuan, H. (2018). Educating culturally responsive Han teachers: Case study of a teacher education program in China. *International Journal of Multicultural Education 20*(2), 42–57, https://doi.org/10.18251/ijme.v20i2.1609.

Zarate, G. & Gohard-Radenkovic, A. (2005). *La reconnaissance des compétences interculturelles.* Paris: Didier.

Acknowledgements

I wish to thank Ning Chen for designing the figure presenting the four conceptual metaphors used in this Element. As always, his talent and perseverance are very much appreciated.

Cambridge Elements ☰

Critical Issues in Teacher Education

Tony Loughland

University of New South Wales

Tony Loughland is an Associate Professor in the School of Education at the University of New South Wales, Australia. Tony is currently leading projects on using AI for citizens' informed participation in urban development, the provision of staffing for rural and remote areas in NSW and on Graduate Ready Schools.

Andy Gao

University of New South Wales

Andy Gao is a Professor in the School of Education at the University of New South Wales, Australia. He edits various internationally-renowned journals, such as International Review of Applied Linguistics in Language Teaching for De Gruyter and Asia Pacific Education Researcher for Springer.

Hoa T. M. Nguyen

University of New South Wales

Hoa T. M. Nguyen is an Associate Professor in the School of Education at the University of New South Wales, Australia. She specializes in teacher education/development, mentoring and sociocultural theory.

About the Series

This series addresses the critical issues teacher educators and teachers are engaged with in the increasingly complex profession of teaching. These issues reside in teachers' response to broader social, cultural and political shifts and the need for teachers' professional education to equip them to teach culturally and linguistically diverse students.

Cambridge Elements ≡

Critical Issues in Teacher Education

Elements in the Series

Interculturality, Criticality and Reflexivity in Teacher Education
Fred Dervin

A full series listing is available at: www.cambridge.org/EITE

Printed in the United States
by Baker & Taylor Publisher Services